GREENLAND

Augsburg

WITHD

Minneapolis, Minne

D1622676

NIDAROS

ICELAND

Leif 1000

BERGEN

Erik 982

Erik 985

Bjarni 986

D

RIKI

Leif 999

Ari Marson 983

Thorhall the Huntsman 1012

TO THE NEW WORLD

THE VIKING EXPLORERS

FREDERICK J. POHL is frequently described as a "geographical detective." A former teacher of English at Ohio Wesleyan University and other colleges, his hobby and interest has always been history. The identification of the site of Leif Erikson's house on Cape Cod climaxes more than twenty-five years of research.

THE VIKING EXPLORERS

by Frederick J. Pohl

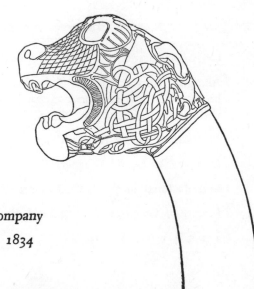

Thomas Y. Crowell Company
New York, Established 1834

Illustrations editor: Rhoda Tripp

Designed by Laurel Wagner

Manufactured in the United States of America

Library of Congress Catalog Card No. 66-12671

1 2 3 4 5 6 7 8 9 10

Acknowledgments

After more than thirty years in the viking field, I remember with gratitude those who generously assisted in the research that went into *The Lost Discovery, The Vikings on Cape Cod, and Atlantic Crossings Before Columbus*. Here I wish to thank those who have helped me in the gathering and arranging of material that has gone into *The Viking Explorers*. Some here named may imagine that they have helped little or not at all, since what they communicated led to negations, as for example, the disappointing discovery that the ax from Mars Head (Tor Bay), Nova Scotia, and the ax in the John Howland House at Plymouth, Massachusetts, are neither of them viking and not even Norse, but are, as their decoration shows, post-Jesuit trade axes. But negatives properly evaluated help guide one to positives.

Archaeologists to whom I am indebted are Glenn A. Black of Indiana University and Angel Mounds; Mr. and Mrs. Robert D. Barnes; F. Newton Miller; Dr. Gad Rausing; Dr. Maurice Robbins; Howard C. Mandell; Edward D. Patterson; Dr. Junius Bird; Frank Kremp; Dr. William A. Ritchie; and Father Michael Wolfe, OMI, Godthaab, Greenland.

Editors have been of invaluable assistance, especially Martin Mann of Thomas Y. Crowell Company, and Mrs. Peter Shepherd. I owe much to conversations and correspondence with Michael Harrington, *Evening Telegram*, St. John's, Nfld.; A. B. Perlin, *Daily Mail*, St. John's, Nfld.; Ken Prentice, Detroit Lakes, Minn.; and Muriel H. Wright, *Oklahoma Historical Quarterly*, Oklahoma City.

Geologists to whom I am most grateful are Professor D. M. Baird, University of Ottawa; Mrs. John D. Frizzell, University of Oklahoma; William E. Ham, Oklahoma Geological Survey; Louis Desjardins, Tulsa, Okla.; and Dr. V. S. Papezik, Memorial University, St. John's, Nfld.

Librarians have been unstinting of their time. I thank especially the attendants at the New York Public Library, and also Miss Mona Cram, Gosling Library, St. John's, Nfld.; Dr. Bruce Ferguson, archivist, St. John's, Nfld.; Dr. F. Eugene Gattinger, Memorial University Library, St. John's, Nfld.; and D. A. Rydewen, library of *Globe and Mail*, Toronto, Ont.

Museum personnel who have been exceedingly helpful are Henry B. Collins, anthropologist at the Smithsonian Institution, Washington, D.C.; Frederick J. Dockstader, curator of the Museum of the American Indian, Heye Foundation, New York, N.Y.; Kristján Eldjárn, director of the National Museum, Reykjavik, Iceland; Allan M. Fraser, provincial archivist and curator of the Newfoundland Museum, St. John's, Nfld.; George McLaren, director of the Provincial Museum, Halifax, N.S.; H. E. Moen, director of the Runestone Museum, Alexandria, Minn.; and Charles R. Strickland, curator of the Pilgrim John Howland Society, Plymouth, Mass.

Professors who have given far more than academic counsel are R. W. Breckenridge, Iowa State University; George F. Carter, Johns Hopkins University; Rhodes W. Fairbridge, Columbia University; Melvin Landon, Nasson College; Leonard B. Loeb, University of California at Berkeley; Bert Salwen, Bennington College; and Cyril Stanley Smith, Massachusetts Institute of Technology.

Property owners who not only gave permission but physically participated in archaeological digging are Mr. and Mrs. Owen R. Gunn and Mr. and Mrs. George M. Paulson, of South Yarmouth, Mass.

Unclassified correspondents and friends, some of whom individually have helped more than anyone, are Robert Barnett, Carthage, Mo.; William A. Bleecker, Anna Maria, Fla.;

Norman H. Cook, Cape Cod (Mass.) Chamber of Commerce; F. M. Cox, town manager, Port-aux-Basques, Nfld.; Mrs. J. Ray Farley, Heavener, Okla.; Ted H. Field, Madison, Wis.; Arthur Godfrey, Pictou, N.S.; Einar O. Hammer, Sons of Norway Society, Minneapolis, Minn.; Robert J. Higgins, Oconomowoc, Wis.; Harold Holand, Milwaukee, Wis.; James L. Hupp, state historian and archivist, West Virginia; Paul N. Jago, North Quincy, Mass.; Richard K. Johnson, South Yarmouth, Mass.; H. J. Kent, Tulsa, Okla.; Victor W. Killick, Sacramento Valley Astronomical Society, Sacramento, Calif.; R. H. Kimball, Lewiston, N.Y.; Thelma M. Kohl, Minneapolis, Minn.; O. G. Landsverk, Glendale, Calif.; A. Lawrence Lovequist, West Dennis, Mass.; K. McGrath, St. John's, Nfld.; Richard L. Mearns, Rochester, N.Y.; Edward O. Mills, New York, N.Y.; Gerald H. Morin, Nashua, N.H.; Peter J. Nelson, Manhasset, N.Y.; Paul Olinkiewicz, Miller Place, N.Y.; William Osborn, Tarrytown, N.Y.; Paul R. Parker, Kennebunk, Me.; Harold Penney, St. Anthony, Nfld.; Calvin Philips, Seattle, Wash.; Holiday Phillips, Coatesville, Ind.; Ernest R. Rankin, Marquette County Historical Society, Marquette, Mich.; Edward Adams Richardson, Bethlehem, Pa.; Leon J. Salter, North Rose, N.Y.; Mr. and Mrs. Fred Scott, St. John's, Nfld.; Major William Smyth, Noank, Conn.; William L. Smyth, Winsted, Conn.; Albert E. Snow, Orleans, Mass.; Nels Snusted, Fergus Falls, Minn.; Most Reverend John E. Taylor, OMI, Oslo; Captain Michael Tobin of the S.S. *William Carson*; Arth J. Tønnesen, Stavanger, Nor.; Mrs. Lydia Wade, Windsor, Conn.; Brigitta Linderoth Wallace, Pittsburgh, Pa.; William Williamson, Camden, Me.

Wise counsel and constant encouragement have come from my wife, Josephine, who by this time has heard enough of the vikings.

Contents

Illustrations

1

Sea Raiders

Black-hulled ships were plowing the North Sea toward the last glow of the sunset. High at the stern of each ship stood a helmsman, bending to the tiller with each heaving wave. The ships carried many armed men, their intent faces framed by helmets with long horns or ravens' wings.

At last one of the lookouts called down from the masthead. He had seen a gleam of lantern light to the west. When the other lookouts had seen it also, all the ships reefed sail. The timing of the crossing had been skillfully planned. June nights are short in the north, and the men had to make their landing during the last hour of darkness.

Their destination was Lindisfarne Island, whose cathedral and shrines were visited by pilgrims from all of England, especially Northumbria. The lantern light was the beacon hung by the monks to warn fishermen of the sand bar that lay between the island and the mainland.

Slowly one ship pulled ahead, and the others followed. The helmeted men murmured together, perhaps we may imagine in words like these: "The island has great treasure of silver and gold—rich booty for us. When we land, speed will be our game and the hammer of Thor. Let us all run fast to the tallest building. Let none stop for the sake of fighting, but if any oppose, strike to kill. Forget not the way back to the ships, and when our leader blows his horn, get back fast."

No Matins or Lauds were sung on Lindisfarne Island that Saturday morning, June 8, 793. At the earliest light of dawn, the sleeping monks and pilgrims were awakened by thuds of splintering, crashing doors. They scarcely had time to set foot to floor before the helmeted men were upon them, wielding ax and sword. Some monks, including the bishop, fled out the postern and hid among the rocks. Others ran into the cathedral, seeking the protection of the high altar. They were slaughtered on the steps of the sanctuary, and the raiders completed the desecration, looting the sacristy and carrying away the chalice, the cross, and other gold and silver. Then the raiders set fire to and burned the cathedral. With songs and laughter they returned to their ships and sailed away.

The raid on Lindisfarne Island is the first viking act of piracy that is recorded in the *Anglo-Saxon Chronicle*. It marks the beginning of three centuries of Scandinavian conquest and domination of sea and land.

The men who attacked Lindisfarne came from the island inlets of the Danes. Together with similar adventurers from the inlets of Norway and Sweden, they were called vikings, from the word *vik*, which in the languages of Denmark and Norway meant inlet or fjord. Because the men of the viks came from several countries and so did not constitute a nation, the word "vikings" is not capitalized.

During the viking period, from the end of the eighth century to almost the end of the eleventh, the sea rovers made themselves the masters of many countries in Europe. The Swedish vikings ravished the Baltic coasts and sailed into the rivers to the east and south.[1] Under a leader named Rus, they developed river-borne carrying of trade goods to and from the Black Sea and Caspian regions, exchanging slaves, bearskins, fox and marten furs, amber and walrus ivory from the north for Byzantine brocades, Arab silver and sword blades, Chinese silks, and other precious objects from as far away as Baghdad.

---

[1] Where the Swedish traders dragged their boats over a portage from the northern streams to the Dnieper, they had to recalk the boat seams. *Smolá* means resin, pitch, tar, and so the place on the Dnieper where they used resin from evergreen trees for recalking became their "tar town"—Smolensk.

Most of the Danish vikings went westward. First they looted isolated island monasteries in England and Ireland. Then they sailed into rivers and pillaged the countryside. They raided Friesland, entered the Rhine and Schelde rivers, overran most of England, and later northwestern France. We can read, if we like, that they brought "nights of horror, the firing of homesteads, slaughter of men, women driven off to slavery or shame, children tossed on pikes." All these things happened. But many vikings, finding trade more profitable than pillage, sought peaceful relations. In Ireland they seized land near the mouth of the Liffey River and built a walled trading town, which was the beginning of the city of Dublin. Similar trading towns became the beginnings of Limerick, Wicklow, Waterford, and other Irish cities. Vikings from Norway attacked the coasts of England, France, Portugal, Spain, and Italy, and in Ireland and France they became more numerous than the Danes. The earls and kings in Scandinavia saw their opportunity and used the viking enthusiasm and thrust for their own territorial ambitions. A surprising number of those who conquered or carved out kingdoms became far-sighted rulers, as Danish vikings eventually did in England, where they had been resisted by King Alfred, and Norwegian vikings (with some Danes) in northwestern France, where they established the dukedom of Northmandy (Normandy). The vikings left a mark on the history of Europe out of all proportion to their numbers.

Yet their more astounding accomplishments were their explorations westward. While most sailors had hugged the shores or steered out of sight of land only across short familiar sea lanes, the vikings turned their prows into the unknown. They ventured across the entire North Atlantic. In the ninth century they colonized the Faeroes and Iceland. In the tenth century they discovered and colonized Greenland. And in the eleventh century they discovered Newfoundland and beyond it to the southwest the great continent they called Vinland. There is evidence that they explored the shoreline south into the Gulf of Mexico. From their home bases in Greenland, they voyaged far into the Arctic, their hunting expeditions undeterred by cold and icy spindrift.

The story of their courage and enterprise was later written down and became part of the Norse sagas (tellings). The colonization of Iceland is related in two documents from the twelfth century: the *Landnamabok* (The Book of the Names of Land-Takers of Iceland) and *Islendingabok* (The Book of the Icelanders), written by Ari Thorgilsson, who was called Ari the Wise. The main sources for the discoveries west of Iceland are the *Flateyjarbok* and the *Hauksbok*. The former, written after 1385, was copied from manuscripts by two priests in Thingeyrar Abbey, a Benedictine monastery about fifteen miles northwest of the home of Icelander Jon Hákonarson, who sponsored the work. One of Hákonarson's descendants who had lived on Flatey, an island in one of Iceland's fjords, presented the volume to the king of Denmark in 1647. As a result, the volume now in the Royal Library in Copenhagen is generally called *Flateyjarbok* (Flat Island Book).

Hauksbok, now in the Arnamagnaean Library in Copenhagen, was written by the lawman Hauk Erlendson, a descendant of Thorfinn Karlsefni, the hero of the book. Erlendson died in 1334. A variant of the narrative, sometimes called "The Saga of Erik the Red," is also in the Arnamagnaean Library. While *Flateyjarbok* was slanted to please Greenland listeners and *Hauksbok* to please Icelanders, both are invaluable.[2] Without them we would be unable to piece together

---

[2] Although the *Flateyjarbok* was written later than *Hauksbok*, many believe that it came more directly from Greenland sources, so that it is sometimes referred to as "The Greenland Saga." The earliest Icelandic manuscripts date from about 1180, and in the fourteenth century old manuscripts of every kind were extensively copied. Since the *Flateyjarbok* and *Hauksbok* were copied from earlier manuscripts, the question of priority between them can have no significance. Previous to the first writing of either of the narratives, the stories of the viking explorations on the western side of the Atlantic had been handed down from generation to generation by oral transmission. My previous books show that the vikings were by no means the first Europeans to cross the Atlantic. The vikings, however, were the first to leave records of explorations on the western side of the ocean.

from the often bewildering relics in Newfoundland and North America the geographical achievements of the vikings. As it is, we can reconstruct the heroic voyages of Erik the Red, Leif Erikson, Thorvald Erikson, and Thorfinn Karlsefni.

Corroborative of the largest claims for viking explorations of North America is a World Map of 1440 now in the Beinecke Library at Yale (see photograph on page 126). This map, which shows Vinland as an immense land southwest of Greenland, was found in 1957 in Europe by Laurence Witten, a New Haven rare book dealer. It is 11 by 16 inches in size, drawn in ink on parchment. It was bound in with twenty-one manuscript pages. But wormholes in the map and in those pages did not coincide. It was concluded that the map had been part of a larger volume. Not long thereafter, by extraordinary happenstance, that larger volume, *Tartar Relation*, came into the possession of Yale Library. Microscopic study showed that wormholes in this volume coincided with those on the map. The map was then studied by cartographers at Yale and at the British Museum and elsewhere. Its genuineness, the authenticity of the handwritten notations on it, and its dating as about 1440 were established beyond question.

On the 1440 World Map, Greenland is remarkably accurate in general outline of what appears to be the whole of it. It certainly shows familiarity with the Greenland west coast from Cape Farvel (60° North) up to at least 77° North, over 1,100 miles of north-south extension. R. A. Skelton, Superintendent of the Map Division of the British Museum, says Greenland on the 1440 map "is an assumed extension from 60° to 83° North." He thus gives it a length of twenty-three degrees of latitude, or 1,585 miles.

Vinland on the 1440 map is pictured as twice the north-south length of Greenland! As explored by Karlsefni (see chapter 13), Vinland began at the northern tip of Labrador, and twice 1,100, or 2,200, miles south of that is the southern tip of Florida! Nothing on the 1440 map of Vinland resembles Hudson Strait which extends from the Atlantic Ocean off the coast of the north end of Labrador for 500 miles to the northwest to the entrance into Hudson Bay. The northern of the two deep indentations in Vinland, a river flowing in a northeast direction from a great lake is obviously the St. Lawrence. Most of the outline of Vinland is drawn with conventional scallops, but the east coast between the two indentations suggests a factual source, its contour being remarkably similar to that of the actual coast for almost a thousand miles south from the St. Lawrence. The southern broad indentation therefore probably represents Chesapeake Bay greatly exaggerated and its main axis in a wrong direction. However, if Skelton's observation regarding Greenland is correct, and if in consequence Vinland on the 1440 map represents over 3,000 miles of north-south extension, the broad indentation may delineate the Caribbean.

Although we know a good deal about the daily lives of these explorers and about the ships they sailed, we can only speculate about what led them to turn their ships westward. The movement was of course part of a general wave of expansion from Scandinavia, and one reason for this was the explosive growth of population throughout Europe toward the end of the eighth century. In Scandinavia a local food shortage, a famine in one of the viks, may have helped turn men to sea roving. Then as the first raiders and later traders returned home with treasures, hundreds and then thousands of Scandinavians, seeking to share their success, became vikings.

But we are nearer to understanding what motivated the vikings to venture into the unknown if we look at the men themselves. The vikings, like adventurers of any period, were alert, energetic, physically able. A popular poem, *Havamal*, described the requisite qualifications this way: "A man who wishes to despoil others of their lives and goods must be up betimes. A loafing wolf never gets fat, a sleeping man never wins a battle." A viking expedition was a call to the courageous, the enterprising and resolute, the imaginative and the farsighted. But it was also a call to the most calculating, cunning, and cruel in human nature. All these qualities are revealed in the great viking explorers whose immortal feats are retold in these pages.

2

At Home in the Viks

Along the viks, wherever the slope of the land permitted, men built their farmhouses and barns, planted their vegetable gardens and grainfields, tended their livestock. Above the dwellings and meadows on the steeper slopes lay orchards and pastures for grazing cattle. Still higher, on slopes too steep for cattle, rose the forest. In the many instances where farms were flanked by sheer cliffs, the folk could reach neighboring farms only by boat. Many of the ancestors of the viking explorers of lands on the western side of the Atlantic were brought up on such farms—most of them on the farms of Norway.

The viks of Norway are warmed by the Gulf Stream. At sea level, even close to glaciers, roses bloom out of doors every month of the year. However, the high, forested slopes are cold, and inland, as well as along fingers of land between fjords, there are ice fields whose glaciers melt into the inner ends of the fjords.

In viking times a typical Norwegian farm could produce enough food for twenty to forty or more persons, but its size and isolation virtually forced it to remain an almost completely self-supporting unit.

Ownership handed down within one family was the custom. When the eldest son married, he had to take on complete legal responsibility for the entire farm—a fact that discouraged him from marrying too young. On his wedding day he and his bride moved into the principal house; his parents moved into the second house, and his grandparents into the third. Brothers and sisters, aunts, uncles, cousins, and various retainers lived in the other houses. This custom of continued ownership by one family grew into law. Today, if an owner for any reason has to sell his farm, any member of the family may buy it back at a fair price established by a judge. Norway boasts of farms that have been owned by the same family for a thousand years—from viking times until now.

The absolute limits nature had set to the size of the farm meant that there was no land for all the younger sons. The population on the farms tended to outgrow the food supply. This is borne out by the persistence of the custom in viking times of exposing or casting into the sea unwanted children. By and large it was the younger sons who felt themselves cooped-up and who dreamed of finding opportunities in other lands. Moreover, these young men were bursting with energy. Perhaps more than any other people, before or since, they scorned the idea of playing safe. This passion for daring adventure as well as a desire for wealth and property was one of the main motivations for viking explorations.

We may find the key at least to the physical strength and endurance of the vikings in the diet the Norwegians enjoyed. While only some 1,047 square miles of their rugged land was suited for agriculture, a Norwegian farm could produce a staggering variety of food. And thanks to the Gulf Stream, some vegetables and cereal grains did better in the fjords of northern Norway than toward the southern end of that country. The vegetables included turnips, kale, cabbages, onions, carrots, peas, lentils, cress. The cereals were wheat (called "corn"), which grew as far as latitude 64° North and up to more than 1,000 feet above sea level; rye, which grew up to 69° North; barley and oats, which grew up to a degree still farther north with a 90-day growing season. The farmers grew hops, and brewed mead, ale, and beer. They picked currants, gooseberries, blackberries, raspberries, strawberries, elderberries, and cloudberries (which look like white raspberries). In their orchards they raised plums, apples, and cherries. They had hazelnuts and walnuts.

The farmers raised horses, cattle, sheep, pigs, goats, and chickens. They kept dogs and cats. Wild animals gave additional variety to Norwegian tables: bear, elk, reindeer, and many birds. They also hunted eiderducks, otters, beaver, wolves, marten, and fox. From the sea they took walruses, seals, dolphins, and whales. They caught fish of many kinds, including cod, haddock, ling, halibut, and turbot, but principally herring. They also fished fresh-water lakes and streams.

The result of all this was a much more varied diet than was enjoyed by any other group of people at this time. One eleventh-century writer, Adam of Bremen, observed that the Swedes had much food of great variety and were, as a result, physically large. He said that by comparison Norway was poorly fed. This was certainly not the case with those people who lived on farms.

In viking times two meals a day were the custom—one in early midmorning, one in the late afternoon. But hungry farm boys did their first raiding in the kitchen quarters or in the orchards. Fieldworkers no doubt had a snack at noon washed down with ale or beer, and maybe folk chewed a bit of smoked herring at other times.

Having the benefit of a stimulating climate as well as all the necessary vitamins and minerals, the Scandinavian farmers were among the healthiest, tallest, and strongest people in Europe. By comparison with other Europeans, the Scandinavians were giants. The average height of a man was five feet eight inches, according to measurements of skeletons from viking burial mounds. This average includes many older men who presumably had lost stature with advanced age. Men in their teens and early twenties are generally one to two inches taller than they are in later years, and since many younger men either died in battles abroad or settled elsewhere and never returned, the absence of their bodies lowers the average.

The viking chiefs who organized raiding parties chose men for agility and strength—and also for their height or, rather, for long sword arms. The stature and weight of individual vikings was a potent fact in their success in hand-to-hand fighting in the countries they invaded.

Moreover, these men had skills, especially in wood and metalworking, which enhanced their usefulness to the group as a whole. In their metalworking, men in Denmark and Norway smelted iron from swamp ores to make tools, agricultural implements, and weapons, but such iron had so many impurities and such low carbon content that it lacked satisfactory hardness. Every man desired superior weapons, and sword blades made by the Arabs or the French were recognized as vastly superior to those of plain bog iron. With use of purer ores from Sweden, some of the Scandinavians were able to make stonecutting tools and swords and battle-axes of the hardness of steel, or they could weld very hard edges on them. Spectroanalysis has revealed that viking weapons and tools had edges that were either steel or close to it in hardness. One Norwegian ruler in the tenth century had a "blue sword." This was blued steel, made by cooling in water the red-hot steel and then tempering it until the surface obtained blueness. Some weapons made in Scandinavia, as well as some obtained from the Arabs or the French, were damascened.

The vikings could fashion all kinds of carpenter's tools: chisels, drills, awls, gouges, and planers. In addition, they made household utensils of ingenious and convenient shapes.

The implements used by the women, such as spinning wheels and looms, needles, scissors, and pressing irons, were in most cases fashioned by men of the family. Most wives cooked with bronze or iron kettles and hung roasts from metal hooks. Farmers working the land used plows, spades, and hoes. They cut their crops with sickles and scythes they had shaped for themselves. When they went fishing they used their own fishhooks, spears, nets, and harpoons. They devised too their own harness, bridles, reins, saddles, stirrups, and spurs, and often decorated these elaborately. Though an occasional traveling metalworker came around to make or repair metal objects, his services were not needed everywhere. Many farms had their own smithy. Certainly, it was easier to shoe a horse at home than to transport the horse by boat to a smith across the fjord.

Primitive houses in Scandinavia had earth walls with upright timbers at the corners to support roofs of wattle, covered with sod or thatch. Where timber was plentiful, farmers made their buildings of wood. Logs could easily be rolled down from the forests to the place where they were needed. Houses were built either with half logs set vertically in what is called stave construction or with full logs laid horizontally. In Sweden and some parts of Norway log houses stood on corner foundations of stone so that the floor was above snowdrifts. Thin boards or planks were little used, for to make a board with ax and adz was a time-consuming and wasteful process. A log had to be split in two, and wood chipped away from each half until a single plank was left. It was more efficient to split a log into several sections and to square each section roughly into a post or beam. There were handsaws to cut pieces to desired length.

The few boards or planks that were laboriously produced by the ax-and-adz chipping process were too valuable for house walls. Instead, they were objects upon which their owners lavished their skill in decorative carving. A houseowner's most prized possessions were the carved bedboards that adorned his family's sleeping platform. In addition, if he were a chieftain, he valued the carved heads of the posts that flanked the high seat in the hall where he presided over his followers.

But it was in boatbuilding that the Scandinavians came nearest to a craft of great artistry. Their specific accomplishments are related in the next chapter.

Although most vikings were farm-bred, a few came from towns or seaport trading centers. There were small market towns where people came to worship and make sacrifices to their gods. Many towns were fortified; a few, such as Trelleborg at the southern tip of Sweden, were military towns. Archaeologists have uncovered at least twenty towns in Scandinavia that were inhabited in viking times. These include Birka, Sigtuna, Skara, and Lund in Sweden; Hedeby, Slesvig,

Aalborg, Aarhus, Odense, Viborg, and Roskilde in Denmark; and Oslo, Bergen, and Nidaros (now Trondheim) in Norway.

In the seaports there was a lively trade in many objects from abroad, such as fine cloth from Friesland and brocades from the Saracens. The Scandinavians prized fine embroidery and the barbaric splendors of jeweled rings, necklaces, bracelets, studded belts, and bright-colored ribbons. These signs of wealth or status helped intensify the desire of young men to acquire property—whether by raids or by trade in other lands.

The vikings developed a characteristic style of art, though their designs were influenced by objects brought in by trade or plunder from other countries. They copied French flower and leaf ornamenation and Irish designs of animals. A few Celtic cross patterns too were imported, apparently several centuries before the Scandinavians became Christianized.

In their designs, the vikings tended to intricately interwoven patterns whose rhythmic quality communicates an aesthetic feeling of over-all unity. This is high praise and well deserved. Such designs might decorate a belt, shield, or the handle of the knife a viking always carried in his belt. The pommel and hilt of a viking sword or its scabbard were often ornamented, but bows and arrows and spears afforded little opportunity for elaborate decoration, and ax handles not much more. The viking craftsmen loved to work in silver, a brighter metal than gold. In fact, many of them prized silver more than gold.

The clothes worn in viking times are known from some burial mounds and from various literary references. The women wore sleeveless underclothes and tunics of short skirts. When the temperature required, they covered themselves with sleeveless woolen capes. One feature of their costume gave some indication of husband's or father's wealth. This was the breast buckle of large and elaborately decorated metal. The kind of metal—whether bronze, iron, gold, or silver—and the kind of decoration reflected the wearer's status.

The men wore close-fitting woolen tunics, held at the waist

by a girdle, and trousers of knee length. They wore woolen
cloaks or capes. One viking was reported to have had "a cape
the hood of which was tied around the neck, and a one-sleeved
cape it was." Many men wore armlets of bronze or silver, em-
bossed with knobs or wrought with an intricate fretwork.
Against cold, both men and women protected head, shoulders,
and back with peaked woolen hoods, which hung down behind
like bags and were no doubt often used as such. Both sexes
wore hides on their feet, tied by thongs at instep and ankle.
Some wore leather pieces stitched together in shoe form.

These clothes gave adequate protection against wind and
rain. At the same time they permitted free use of the limbs.

While interest in and desire for material things influenced
these people of the north, their character was molded also by
less tangible things, such as religion and tradition.

In the northern summer the long hours of daylight left
no time in the evenings for anything but sleep. In winter,
however, when less work could be done, the long evenings
were given to entertainment. The Scandinavians played chess
and checkers and similar games. Around the fireplace they recounted tales of their heroes and gods, sang, and drank toasts
to the gods and each other.

The tales were so often retold that most hearers knew
every word. History lived only in these memorized oral accounts, repeated from generation to generation. In viking times
most Scandinavians could not read or write, though a few
knew the runic alphabet acquired from Germanic tribes.
Runic letters were borrowings, with modifications, from the
Greek and Roman alphabets, which the Germanic tribes
encountered in the second century. Early Germanic runic
writing had twenty-four letters, which were listed not in
alpha-beta order but beginning with the six letters: F U Th
A R K. By viking times the old futhark had been simplified to
sixteen letters.

The illiterate majority thought that the rare persons who
knew the futhark were in command of the supernatural. The

Scandinavians believed the runemasters could weave spells. Runic inscriptions were supposed to be a potent charm against evil. They were a form of magic whose maker held status because he could interpret them. Some men rewarded runemasters handsomely for putting good luck writing on swords and axes. To enhance his superiority, a runemaster sometimes used abbreviations, omitting one of the strokes of a letter, or omitting a letter altogether. As a result, the best any other runemaster could do would be to guess at the meaning. A sacred pattern was often followed with a prescribed number of letters to a line. The runemaster frequently added artistic decorations to the stone surface upon which he carved. Some runic inscriptions were prayers, some were incantations, some were spells to bring luck in hunting, many were grave markers. A very few, the most valuable to us, were brief historic records.

We know little with certainty about the religion of the viking times. What we do know of the Norse gods is seen only through thick lenses of centuries of Christian overlay, of gradual changes in the gods as they too became partly Christianized. For centuries after the Scandinavian countries officially accepted Christianity, the people held to the old religion. Opposition to Christianity continued for 150 years in Denmark, 200 years in Norway, and 300 years in Sweden. From its very persistence we know that the Norse religion had satisfying metaphysical elements.

The chief of the gods was Odin, or Wodin, who was supposed to command the obedience of the other gods, but sometimes failed to. He was nevertheless their ruler—and the favorite god of human rulers and of the intellectually "advanced." Odin reflected the character of rulers and clever men. A ruthless aristocrat, capricious and uncharitable, he was reputed to have great wisdom. Odin was married to Frigg.

Thor, one of Odin's sons, was the most widely beloved of the gods. He reflected the character of the common man. Though he had a sense of humor, he was not skilled in subtle tricks and ingenious schemes like his father. He was hasty in

judgment and had an ill-controlled temper. When Thor rode
on top of the clouds in a cart pulled by goats, the pounding of
their hoofs and the rumble of the cart wheels were thunder. He
was the rain-bringer and therefore the farmer's god. He was
also the god of fisherfolk and sailors. With his mighty hammer, he was particularly the god of smiths, of metalworkers,
and he was a protector against giants (the hostile forces of
nature). He was a benevolent guest at peasant weddings. Some
of his adventures were less than dignified, but that made him
all the more human. He had two sons, Magui and Modi, whose
names meant "strength" and "courage."

Frey was god of fertility, the most inexplicable of all
mysteries. His sister Freya was goddess of love and beauty.
Tyr, or Tiw, was god of war. The names of these gods persist
in the English language in four days of the week. Hel was the
female keeper of most of the dead, and her ice-cold dwelling,
with addition of an ell, became an ample home for Christian
sinners and heretics. The Christians installed central heating.
There were of course many other lesser gods, each with a
definite character.

Heroes who died on the battlefield went to Valhalla, a
paradise of pork feasting and heady potions. But inevitably
they expected to take up their weapons again in the final battle
of the world. In that last war everything was destined to be
destroyed. Then a new era would begin with a new race of
men who would be happy and would live under just laws. In
this renewal of humanity we perceive a Christian interpola-
tion.

Above all things, the religion of the vikings stressed
courage. And the vikings glorified the way heroes of past gen-
erations had faced death. A hero who was only wounded in
battle had lost an immediate opportunity of entering Valhalla.
However, he still had a way to reach the feasting tables. He
could refuse a "straw" death (in a bed) and have himself laid
within his ship. Then after raising sail, his followers would set
the hull afire and from the shore sing paeans of war and triumph until hero and ship went down in flames.

Though this custom was discontinued because of the rising cost of ships, the vikings treasured the romantic tradition of death by ship-burning, and their descendants still do. On the night of the second Tuesday in January at Lerwick in the Shetland Islands, people celebrate the old custom. The replica of a viking ship is drawn through the streets accompanied to its launching by hundreds of men with flaming torches.

When the procession comes to rest at the shore, young and old lift up their heads and sing a war song: "The Norseman's Home." Then the elected leader of the masqueraders, resplendent in purple robes and crimson breeches, wearing martial winged-helmet, leaves the ship with shield and battle axe in hand. At the sound of a trumpet hundreds of flaming torches are hurled through the darkness into the ship which becomes a sheet of flame. This is indeed a bonfire! [1]

With voluntary immolation by fire, the vikings affirmed that the hero would find happiness in permanent release from the body. Cremation was associated with the most ideal aspects of paganism, and this was no doubt one of the reasons why the Church always insisted upon burial. To shrink from death was unmanly, so Christianity's offer of escape from the fear of death could have tempted a viking very little.

However, though Scandinavians scorned showing any fear of death, they feared spells and evil magic. Some vikings carried rattles, apparently to frighten away witches or malevolent spirits. Rattles were buried with their owners, presumably for protection in the realm of ghosts. The rattle consisted of an iron bar about seven or eight inches long, from which "hung several rings and sometimes small bells, i.e., objects that rattle or tinkle when shaken. . . . Nothing certain is known of the use of these rattles. They seem to have had some connection with riding and traction harness and are sometimes explained

[1] "Yo Helly AA," Lerwick *Family Herald and Weekly Star*, Jan. 28, 1954, p. 32.

as the sleigh-driver's or the horseman's magic rattle for keeping evil spirits at a distance." [2] In later less superstitious times when men rode in horse-drawn sleighs over snow, their harness carried jingling bells—not to ward off demons but to give warning of an otherwise soundless but speedy approach. It is interesting that fewer rattles of viking times have been found in burials in western Norway than in eastern Norway, where there is more snow.

Though the possession or acquisition of wealth was usually a trustworthy sign of a god's favor, there were several virtues valued above riches. Adam of Bremen said he found the Scandinavians "though bound by heathen error, more honorable and hospitable than any other people." Generosity and hospitality along with truthfulness and bravery were considered supreme qualities of goodness.

Religious practices included meetings at temple towns, where there was spattering of blood with sacrifices and the eating of meat that had been offered to idols. In temple towns, such as Uppsala, in Sweden, and Maeren, in Norway, the great religious festivities must in other respects have resembled what we would call a country fair. However, at Uppsala, the traditional early home of the Norse gods, there was a great festival every nine years, at which horses and dogs and nine men, probably slaves, were sacrificed and hung in a grove. The temple at Uppsala had three great idols of Odin, Thor, and Frey, in that order, with Thor in the middle. Frey, now the god of the sophisticated, had a mighty phallus.

We are ignorant of many viking customs. We do know that on the evening of the first day in May they lit the fires of spring and danced round these bonfires to celebrate the end of winter. They joined all nature in welcoming the sun with other joinings also.

Fertility was a complete mystery before people understood the relation between copulation and pregnancy. Since a woman could give birth, something no man could do, men

[2] Johannes Brøndsted, in *Annual Report of the Smithsonian Institution,* 1953, pp. 377–78.

were in awe of women. To bolster their egos, men treated women as strange creatures with whom it was unwise to share one's innermost thoughts. Within the aura of mystery, in spite of their one superiority of function, women were not recognized as equals. However, with more understanding, men's view of women changed. The vikings expressed their understanding in a popular story. The wandering god Rig comes to the dwelling of some serfs, Oldefar and his wife Oldemor. Rig is welcomed and he gets into bed with them and stays three days. Nine months later Oldemor bears a son. Then Rig comes to the farm of Bedstefar and his wife Bedstemor, and is warmly received. He gets into bed with them and stays three days. Nine months later Bedstemor has a child. And then Rig visits the home of the nobles Far and Mor, is hospitably entertained, gets into bed with them and stays three days. Nine months later Mor bears a son. The tale shows that serfs, peasants, and nobles are all alike.

Home life in Scandinavia contributed to man's changing views of women. When a man came in from the cold and wind, he sat as close as he could to the hearth where his wife was busy. He could not avoid observing her useful activities. What she was doing made sense. As he began to talk with her, he found he could defer to her judgment in some of his problems. She naturally became his helpmeet.

Viking women had a right to divorce, and the *Landnamabok* shows they could legally hold property. A man in Iceland named Geirrod gave his sister Geirrid a homestead. "She built her dwelling right across the highway, and she sat upon a stool and invited in guests, and a table within stood ready with meat upon it." Also, Thorun, a woman in Iceland, "owned land down to Videlaek, to where it joined the land of her sister Thurid, the soothsayer, at Grof." Johannes Brøndsted asserts that among the chieftains and landowners, but not the serfs, "women enjoyed high esteem and full freedom." Of course in an age of brutality it was still a man's world, and men quoted the maxim we find in the popular poem *Havamal:* "Do not trust a woman's words, be she single or married: their hearts run on wheels, they are a prey to moods." Most slaves were women captives from abroad. And there was prejudice against women as rulers. The first woman to become a ruler in Scandinavia was Queen Margareta in the fourteenth century, who inherited the thrones of Denmark, Sweden, and Norway. To meet the prejudices of Scandinavians, she set up an adopted son as puppet king.

In viking times governmental power was vested in two institutions: the monarchy and the lawthing. A man aspiring to the throne—even the rightful heir—had to appear before a great gathering of landowners. He made a kind of campaign speech and the landowners went through the form of electing him. The king-elect then made promises and his subjects pledged their obedience. On at least one occasion in the tenth century a large group of small landowners refused what one of the kings of Norway asked, using the phrase "our freedom." So it appears that in viking times the supreme power was occasionally in the hands of the freeholders.

By viking times the freeholders were no novices in government. Their ancestors had inhabited the Scandinavian peninsula for thousands of years, and their customs had grown from remote antiquity. In every district or petty kingdom there was a lawthing. This was an out-of-doors meeting at a site set apart for the purpose. The site might be a little island in a lake, or some plateau in a valley. Within that area, as in a modern courtroom, legal discussions were held, suits were heard, disputes were adjudged, and men were tried for crimes. Laws were also proclaimed. The meeting was always well attended; there would be sports and contests of skill and strength nearby, and buying and selling as at a country fair, and, of course, some worship of the gods.

When a legal decision was proposed, assent was signified not by shouts or show of hands but by banging of shields or the rattling of spears. Decreed punishments included fines, exile, death, or slavery. Of these, exile was the most dreaded. Landless young men who persistently made trouble were exiled for a stated time. Almost invariably they became sea rovers.

Decisions of the lawthing were enforced not by any

official action but by the pressure of public opinion. When an offender was convicted, the aggrieved person or family saw to it that the sentence was carried out. In other words, the law-thing authorized the plaintiff to take the law into his own hands. Sometimes a suspected person was ordered to undergo an ordeal by fire, or the two parties to a quarrel were ordered to a duel on some island, in what was called a *Holmgang* (Islandgoing). Lawthings made Scandinavians very fond of legal processes and excessively litigious. On the positive side, they also instilled an intense awareness of the importance of law as well as respect for it.

In any gathering, when talk turned to serious discussion, it was held to be a quality of wisdom in a man if he appeared to be very deliberate, if not what we would call slow, in his expression of an opinion. Aphorisms in *Havamal* indicate that a man was judged by his utterance, which was felt to be the revelation of his soul. He knew his every word would be weighed by his hearers, after which they would respect or disparage him. Derision by sarcasm was often near the lips. Men boasted of their manly qualities and courage, and it became the talk habit to express a strong desire to excel and even die in battle. Such words no doubt stirred in boy listeners a will to perform deeds like those by which their elders had won applause.

Boys and young men absorbed these and other values from observing their elders. A boy brought up on a farm knows how material losses result from carelessness. He acquires the habit of heeding what is ordered by elder and wiser heads. A boy learns the same lesson in a fishing boat. Accustomed to discipline, he has a well-developed sense of his own responsibility to any enterprise as a whole. He knows that the lives of the entire group depend on the co-operation of every man. Such boys become men who realize the importance of unquestioning obedience in war—and viking raids were a kind of war.

3

Viking Ships

Down nearly to viking times, Scandinavian boats had no sails, even though sails had been used for more than two thousand years in the Mediterranean. Carvings of Stone Age and Bronze Age boats, together with later archaeological finds, reveal the slow development in boatbuilding from hollow log canoes to ocean-going ships.

In the narrow twisting viks of western Norway the high mountain walls shut out most winds, leaving the surface of the waters calm and unruffled. Sails there were of little use. What was needed was a light boat, one that could easily be hauled up among the rocks. Centuries before the viking era, men made flat-bottomed boats of hides stretched over a light wooden frame. These boats resembled Eskimo umiaks, except that they had obliquely protruding prow and sternposts. The posts served several purposes. They kept the frame and hide covering from banging into rock walls; they furnished a solid handhold at each end of the boat; they served as levers to raise the center of the boat off a submerged obstacle or a shallow; and finally, they made good handles for lifting and carrying the boat ashore—a feature particularly useful along banks of pebbles or gravel.

The men of the viks paddled their skin boats with sticks to which they had affixed pieces of oxhide or sealskin at the water ends. Later they used oars. The skin boats were light enough to ride the crest of waves. They were flexible enough to bend and yield rather than break under wave pressures. But

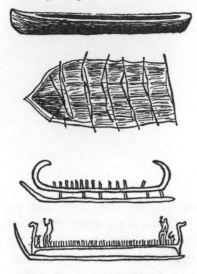

The first Scandinavian boats were hollowed-out log canoes (top) as shown in the author's sketch. Then people made light, flat-bottomed skiffs of hides stretched over a flexible wooden frame. Protruding prow- and stern-posts, as well as extended false keels (bottom two sketches), made good handles for lifting and kept the boats from damage by rocks.

if the boats were dragged and not lifted ashore, the unprotected skin of the hull would be ripped on sharp rocks. It was discovered that if a false keel were attached to the end posts, the boat could safely be hauled ashore, even if heavily loaded with fish. This was the primary purpose and advantage of the false keel. A further advantage was discovered when the men went fishing near the mouths of the fjords. In the strong winds and currents in the broad reaches there, the false keel tended to prevent sideslipping and unmanageable turnings and so helped to hold the boat on a steady course. The innovation was soon widely adopted.

Fishermen in flat-bottomed skin boats fitted with false keels fished around all the islands off the western coast of Norway. Some ventured far out into the ocean beyond sight of land. As early as the sixth century fishermen had adventured across the several hundred miles of ocean as far west as the Hebrides. Inevitably they got to know the Shetlands, Orkneys, and the north coast of Scotland.

The intrepid fishermen discovered of course what every boy learns who plays around with a canoe or rowboat—when there is a following wind, the boat will go fast if the rower stands near the bow with his back to the wind, or if he holds up an oar or paddle so that its blade catches the wind. The fishermen desired some kind of wind-watching device. In a skin boat it was obviously impossible to set up a mast to support a sail. For men with woodworking skill and plenty of timber available along the seacoast, an attempt to build a hull all of wood was inevitable. Then the keel, as a constructional part of the boat, would be strong enough to bear the weight of a mast. However, a wooden hull would weigh much more than a hide-covered frame; it was essential that the bottom and sides of the wooden hull should be as light as possible to offset the heavy keel. But the builders soon discovered that if an all-wood boat were made after the model of a skin boat, the bottom would have to be thick and heavy to avoid breaks. Someone then hit upon the idea of an arched or rounded bottom, which could be made much thinner and was also stronger than a flat bottom. This led to the idea of making a frame in the form of curved ribs. Of comparatively thin timbers, the ribs were laboriously carved into curved form. Later men learned how a straight piece could be steamed and bent to hold permanently the required curve. Over the ribs the builders laid thin planks longitudinal to the length of the vessel. Planks somewhat less than an inch in thickness were found about right. Thicker than that was unnecessary, and thinner was not strong enough.

The development of Scandinavian boatbuilding was a natural evolutionary process.

It has been suggested that a Mediterranean ship, evolved from the Phoenician-Arabian type, wrecked or captured in a fjord, provided a model for the Norwegians. Such an arrival of a Mediterranean ship could have happened. But we do not know that it did, nor do we have any reason to suppose that it did. There was no sudden jump in the development of wooden boatbuilding by the Norsemen. If a Mediterranean ship was available for study, it certainly was not copied by the Norsemen. At most, some of its features would merely have confirmed the Norwegian boatbuilders' own experience in devising their own type of ship.

The men in the viks built from the keel out along the

bottom of the hull and up the sides. They soon discovered the usefulness of having each plank not just set close edge to edge with the next, but shaped to overlap the preceding plank, or strake as it is called, in a construction called clinker-building. By this ingenious overlapping outward from the keel, the boatbuilder got an angled surface of contact between the strakes. He calked the junctures with wool fiber impregnated with tar, and fastened the strakes together with treenails, and later iron nails or bolts.

In somewhat the way earlier builders had tied hides to the frames of skin boats at regular intervals with withies or strings dipped in tar, the Norwegian builder tied the strakes to the ribs. He left bulges for these fastenings along the strake as he carved it. The thin hull was amazingly strong and flexible; either end of the ship could yield to a wave and bend or twist several inches without breaking or producing a leak. The keel and thwarts were straight, but all other pieces of wood that formed the hull were curved. In shaping the ship for efficiency in cutting through the water and rising over waves, the craftsmen produced vessels as perfect as human ingenuity could contrive and with extraordinarily beautiful lines.

As the Norwegians built more wooden-hulled boats, they made still further improvements, which also were widely adopted in the viks. To give greater strength where it was most needed, the strakes at the waterline and the strakes pierced for oarholes were almost twice as thick as the other strakes. The topmost strakes were reinforced by a heavy gunwale. Thwarts strengthened the hull from inside. Oarholes were furnished with shutters that could be closed when the ship was under sail. In some ships, each oarhole had side slits through which the blade end of the oar could be drawn inboard, while an enlargement of the oar handles prevented the oar from slipping out through the hole and thus being lost through negligence.

The keel in cross section was taller than it was wide. This meant that the vessel had a level, horizontal timber on which to be drawn ashore over log rollers. A beam was added to strengthen the keel where it had to support the weight of a mast. A museum guide to a ship of viking time describes the mast-block as "carved in the shape of a fishtail at both sides and through a large hole in this the mast was stepped into a groove in the lowest beam. When the mast was stepped the open back part of the hole in the mast-block was closed by means of a large oak plug. When this was removed the opening was large enough to permit the mast being lowered toward the stern."

Like the primitive skin boats, the ships of viking times were double ended. The ends of the curving planks were snugly fitted into dowels in the stout end posts. There were thus only five heavy timbers in a ship of viking times: the keel, the mast, the mast-block, the stempost or prowpost, and the sternpost. Most hulls were made of oak, and the masts of pine.

The mast of a viking ship was about thirty-five feet tall. A lookout man viewing the water from this height could see the horizon at least seven and one-half miles away. The mast bore a yard from which hung a single square sail, broader at the bottom than the top. The sail was raised and lowered by a windlass. The sail usually was made of wadmal, and was often striped red and white. The mast was slightly abaft of amidships. This meant that the wind pressure against the sail tended to push the stern sideways more than it did the prow, thus helping to keep the prow pointed in relation to the wind direction. Sailing into the wind by a viking ship was sometimes possible, but was very inefficient, and so on old maps on many a promontory far out from a harbor along the western coast of Norway we find the descriptive term *Stad*, a protected place for ships to ride at anchor while waiting for a fair wind. Forward of the mast on each gunwale was a device to receive and hold the end of a spar, a tacking boom called a *beitiáss*, to make it possible to "beat" into the wind. Only one of these booms was used at any one time, its outer end holding taut the lower corner of the forward edge of the sail. When the boom was adjusted and lashed into position, it kept the sail spread to catch more wind. With this device the ship could sail slightly into the wind, no more than one point, but side-drifting away from the wind lost most of the progress made. The horizontal keel helped hold the ship to a straight course.

The use of a sail required a steering device. This was a pole with a board or blade at its end. Held in the water deeper than the keel, like a centerboard, it helped keep the ship from drifting sideways. At right angles to the upper end of the pole, an arm extended inboard for the steersman to handle. By custom the rudder was placed on the right side of the ship, which came to be called the steering board, or starboard, side. The left side, the one brought against a wharf for loading and unloading, was the port side.

The stempost and sternpost of a viking ship were very tall, some up to twelve or fifteen or more feet, and upon their upper ends could be placed carved wooden heads of dragons, serpents, horses, and the like. These toppieces could be un-stepped or folded down. They were never stepped while the ship was at sea because their weight at that height would dangerously accentuate the rolling of the ship. The carved monster-head was displayed only when the vikings entered a port, either to terrify intended victims or, in home ports, to identify the ship and its owner. In enemy ports as protection against stones, arrows, or spears, the vikings also attached rows of shields outside the bulwarks, hanging them over the tholes by their grip straps. Meticulous artists such as Gordon Grant have pictured viking ships under sail at sea with such rows of shields, but the lower edge of the sail might knock off some of the shields, and would certainly do so whenever the sail was lowered, and the shields would not have been hung overboard during rough weather, when waves might sweep them away.

The *hafskips* (ocean ships) that carried the first viking raiders differed from the narrow warships that were used exclusively in inland waters. The *hafskips* were broader and had a higher freeboard. The vikings did not use warships. They never sought naval battles in their raiding ships; the records tell of but two or three viking battles at sea and, in these rare instances, the vikings had no other choice. The raiders relied on sail and used oars only when the wind failed or when maneuvering close to land. Speed was not a major concern to the raiders so long as they were fast enough to escape pursuers. Warships, on the other hand, were designed for pursuit. Peter Nelson of Manhasset, Long Island, who owned one of the three replicas of viking ships built in Norway for the film The Vikings, says his ship's horizontal keel tended to make it difficult to turn the vessel. By contrast, the keel of the Gokstad ship, a warship, was a foot deeper in the middle than toward the ends, and allowed quick pivoting.

The Gokstad ship is one of three warships whose remains have been found well preserved in wet blue clay burials at Tune, Gokstad, and Oseberg. From sixty to seventy-six feet long, with a freeboard of only three feet nine inches, these ships were not designed to defy ocean waves. They were propelled by oars—the Oseberg ship by fifteen pairs, and the Gokstad by sixteen pairs. The pride of Norway, these ships, which date from A.D. 800–900, have been carefully restored and are on display at the famous ship museum at Oslo. Since these were for use in inland waters, and since the vikings were only those men who engaged in sea roving, these warships, though of viking times, cannot, strictly speaking, be called viking ships.

On the western side of Oslo Fjord, Norway, fifteen ship graves were unearthed at Kaupang. The ships themselves have disintegrated, but nearby the imprint of an entire ship of viking times was discovered. The wood had all rotted away, but hundreds of iron nails in the soil clearly revealed the ship's outline. Objects buried with the owners of the ships included a battle-ax, a spear, a shield, a scythe, and a soapstone bowl. Many of the objects found in and around the graves came from foreign lands: an English sword; fragments of textiles from Friesland; a bronze bowl with runic inscription, most likely from Ireland; and several chains of colored beads from other countries.

As time went on, the warrior-carrying raiding ships of the

vikings evolved into cargo-carrying traders, broader and deeper than the raiders. These are known as knörr or knarr. The cargo amidships was covered with oxhide. These ships had only two or three pairs of oars at each end. This was the type of ship on which the vikings braved the entire expanse of the North Atlantic.

Since their lives were dependent on their ships, the vikings took the best possible care of them. They coated hulls with tar as a protection against teredos (shipworms). Wherever a viking crew spent a winter, they hauled up their ship and put it under cover of a shed or roofing of thatched turf. For protection while afloat, a viking ship carried some sort of anchor. In most cases it was a rock tied securely at the end of a rope, though this was probably not heavy enough to hold a ship in a strong wind. A wealthy shipowner might have had a delicately shaped metal anchor, though such an anchor was too slight to hold a ship in a big blow. Ships were in greatest danger near shore, for an uncontrolled swing of a thin-hulled viking ship against a rock could knock a hole in her and sink her. Like all seamen, the vikings had three ways to hold a ship afloat. They could have it "anchored," in which case it could swing with wind, current, and tide. They could "berth" it side-on to a wharf or the shore. They could "moor" it, by having ropes hold it at both ends to prevent it from swinging and touching the shore. In mooring, the natural procedure is to anchor the ship with the prow pointed away from shore, and to run a hawser from the stern to the shore.

A viking ship carried wooden casks or buckets to hold drinking water, and probably a chest to hold valuables. The use of an awning to catch rain water has been recorded. The awning was a waterproof cargo covering, probably of hides or sealskins. There is also a recorded mention of a lad in a viking boat who "lay in the prow, and was in a seal-bag which was drawn together at the neck." This was a waterproof sleeping bag. Each member of a crew no doubt had two such bags, one to sleep in and one to keep his gear dry.

A ship carried a gangplank twenty or more feet long. The

top surface of it was carved out in order to leave protruding transverse ridges that kept a man from slipping when the plank was steeply inclined. Ocean-going ships, thirty to seventy feet long, usually carried an afterboat lashed upside down over the cargo. The afterboat was large enough to hold six to ten or more men, or about half the crew, if needed in an emergency. A small two-man skiff was carried inside the afterboat.

When navigating out of sight of land, the vikings used all available clues to find their positions and steer toward their destination. By observing the shadows of the gunwale on the thwarts at noon, they could hold a course at approximately the same latitude throughout an east-to-west ocean voyage—even though they did not think of latitude in degrees.

From the tenth century on, there is abundant evidence of Icelanders' knowledge of practical astronomy. In the early eleventh century Oddi Helgason, called "Stjörnu Oddi"—Star Oddi, worked out a table of the sun's azimuth and made some surprisingly accurate observations of the sun's declination. His observations of the sun's altitude were expressed not in degrees, but in halft hvéle *(half-wheel) or half-sun's diameter.*[1]

In addition to steering by dead reckoning, the vikings found birds an important guide, especially when approaching land or looking for an island they might otherwise fail to find. Some species of birds fly far out to sea, and some only a few miles. Some birds remain all night at sea, sleeping on the water, but others start back to land before dark. When the birds start early, a mariner knows that the land is farther away than if they start late. The vikings knew their birds and carefully observed the directions of their flights. Even when there was no visibility, the voices of birds could give a mariner essential information. Captain Bob Bartlett, born in New-

[1] G. F. Marcus, in *Mariner's Mirror* (London). Vol. 39, No. 2 (May, 1953), p. 121.

foundland, had a mariner's knowledge of birds; he could tell in a dense fog from the sounds of birds whether he was in the order of twenty miles or two miles or only a quarter of a mile from the shore of Newfoundland.

At night the vikings steered by the moon and stars, but if the sky were overcast, they could fairly well hold their course by the angle direction of waves in relation to the ship, assuming that the wind remained steady. They observed a change of direction in the wind by the appearance of cross wavelets over the large waves.

Even the fog helped some of the vikings to navigate, for those who sailed in the North Alantic learned the locations of prevailing fog banks. Whales had regular fishing banks where plankton were plentiful. The vikings observed the usual locations in which whales and ice floes appeared, and near Greenland they observed the color and temperature of the water. The viking skill in navigation without astrolabe or compass seems almost uncanny.

4

The Settlement of Iceland

"Before Iceland was peopled by the Northmen," the *Landnamabok* tells us, "there were in the country those men whom the Northmen called 'Papas.' These were Christian men, who would not remain here among heathens, and the people believed that they came from the West [Ireland] because Irish books and balls and crosiers were found after they left, and still more things by which one might know that they were West-Men [Irish] that were found in the island of Easter Papay and in Papyli." During the great expansion of missionary activity from Ireland, monks reached Iceland. They had established themselves before the end of the eighth century on islands off the southeast coast.

Iceland was probably known to the ancient Greeks. It seems to have been the island Pytheas, in the fourth century B.C. called Ultima Thule. It was known to the Romans, for several coins, including one minted during the reign of the Emperor Diocletian (284-305), have from time to time been unearthed in Iceland.

Norwegian vikings began visiting Iceland in the ninth century. About 860, a man named Haddod, who had been outlawed from Norway, set sail for the Faeroes. His ship was carried west and he came to a great land. Seeing snow fields, he named the place Snowland, and returned to tell of it in the Faeroes. Gardar, a Swede, having heard about the land, ventured out to see it. By sailing around it he discovered it was an island. He named it Gardarsholme (Gardar's Island).

31

Then Floki Vilgerdsson, a Norwegian, who had heard of Gardarsholme, took some livestock in his ship and sailed far westward, hoping to find and to explore the island. He very cleverly took three ravens to help navigate. When he had been long out of sight of land, he released one of the birds. The raven rose high aloft and circled, and flew back toward Norway. Floki knew there was no land near him ahead, and he sailed on westward. After several days he released another raven. This one flew to a tremendous height in large circles, seeking land in every direction, and then it returned to the ship. That raven was apparently injured or killed in the attempt to recapture it, for thereafter Floki had only one raven. Finally, after several more days, he released the last raven, which rose and promptly flew away westward. Then Floki knew the bird had seen land, and steering in the direction of its flight, came to Gardarsholme. Thereafter he was called Floki the Raven. He found Horn, a good harbor on the southeast coast. He explored the south and the west coasts and entered a wide bay (Breidifjörd) which "so abounded in fish, they gave no heed to gathering in of hay, so that all the livestock perished in the winter."

On the north side of Breidifjörd in Vatnsfjörd (Lake Fjord), Floki and his men erected a homestead shed (*skalitoft*) and a shed to protect their ship from the snows. The remains of the rectangular foundations of the turf walls of the sheds and the stone fireplace in one of them were visible for more than 250 years. Icelanders revered these remains as the homestead of the first viking to winter on the island, and the man who coined its name. The waters around the shores of Iceland do not freeze. But from a mountain Floki saw to the north of it a fjord full of drift ice. Therefore he renamed the island Iceland. Floki was a realist, for back home in Norway he spoke ill of Iceland. However, Thorolf, one of his companions, reported that in Iceland butter dropped from every blade of grass, and thereafter he was called Thorolf Smjör—Thorolf Butter.

The Norwegians colonized Iceland from about 870 to

910. Norway was in constant turmoil as the kings of various regions battled for power. About 860 (some say 862) a ten-year-old boy named Harald became the king of an important district. He reigned "seventy winters," dying in 930 or 933. As a youth, he wanted to marry Gyda, daughter of King Erik of Hordaland, and she said she would accept him only after he became king of all Norway. And so he swore this oath: "I will not cut my hair or comb it until I have gotten to me all Norway." His ambition met strong resistance. As he began to crush opposition, some chieftains chose to leave the country. About four hundred families, who by their reports were the "best" in Norway, fled from King Harald. A few settled in the Faeroes, but most of them, having heard of the butter-fat fields, went to Iceland.

King Harald forced the Orkneys and Shetlands to accept his overlordship, and eventually he got the girl, for he succeeded in uniting all Norway under his rule. During the ten or twelve years of fighting before he cut and combed his hair, he was called Shockhead, but afterward he was called Haarfager—Fairhair.

The Iceland colonists found a bleak land. Although the island was large, about three hundred miles from east to west, and almost two hundred miles from north to south, its interior was mostly uninhabitable. Volcanoes, lava beds, snow peaks, ice fields, and glaciers abounded. There were catastrophic earthquakes and floods. There were earthquake fissures from some of which smoke rose. The name of the principal town, Reykjavik, means "Creek of Smoke." There were hot springs, though no one found any use for them at first. A large part of the food of Icelanders came from birds' eggs and from sea fish: cod, herring, haddock, and halibut. Seals and whales were plentiful, and there were wildfowl, including eider duck. Although there were no navigable rivers, there were some small streams which salmon ascended, and there was some trout fishing. One stream was called Warm Brook.

Running in from the seacoast to the hills of volcanic ash, there were forests of dwarf birch, few more than ten feet tall. But the trees were soon cut down and the land planted to food crops. In one place wood had been so abundant that one of the first settlers "built from it a seagoing ship." Within a very few years the colonists had exhausted supplies of timber, including the large trunks of trees occasionally found in driftwood. Although the climate was tempered by ocean-warmed atmosphere, agriculture was restricted to hardy oats, some root vegetables, and grasses which fed sheep and cattle. Undeniably, some butter did come out of the fields. Lichen, mosses, and sedges grew profusely, and there were some berry-bushes.

A vivid picture of the colonists is given in *Landnamabok*. When Ingolf, their leader, sighted Iceland, "he cast overboard his high-seat pillars for an omen, and he made the vow that he would settle there wherever his high-seat pillars came ashore." He no doubt had observed a set of tide toward shore before he risked his valued carved pieces, and he had some eye as to what land looked good from where he cast them overboard. To co-operate with the gods was legitimate. The pieces came ashore at what came to be called Ingolf's Head, on the south shore. That is where Ingolf first landed, but he improved on the gods' choice, for "Ingolf's Fell west of Ölfus River is where he afterward took land. Ingolf was the most renowned of the settlers, for he came to an uninhabited land and was the first to set up an abode, and the others who settled there afterward did so induced by his example."

Hjorlief, another chieftain, settled farther to the west. He constructed two *skali* (sheds, buildings) 18 fathoms (111 feet) and 19 fathoms (117 feet) long. Though he had an ox, he made the mistake of having his Irish slaves draw the plow. The slaves in time murdered Hjorlief and his men, and fled by boat with the women and chattels to some islands toward the southwest. Ingolf, who ascribed this event to Hjorlief's failure to sacrifice to the gods, went to the islands and killed all the slaves. Because the slaves were Irish, the islands were called Westman's Islands.

The great majority of the earliest Icelanders were Thor

worshipers. They believed that the earth-fires, volcanic eruptions, showed the wrath of the gods. They called a man and his son "the godless, because they would not sacrifice, but trusted to their own might." There was one Christian viking who, as his envious heathen neighbors noted, had a brook full of fish. When they ousted him from his land, his former brook had no fish, but the brook on his new holding had many. The same thing happened each time he was forced to move. Also, a river opened itself a new channel that advantaged another Christian. Superstitions worked for both religions.

The names of some of the settlers give glimpses into their lives: Thraud the Much Sailing, Thorgeir Cutcheek, Hard Hitter, Thorstein Snowshoes, Aud the Deep-Minded, Thord the Yeller, Madpate and his son Scum, Ketil Broadsole, Ulf the Squinter, Odd the Gaudy, Thrand Spindleshanks, Ljot the Unwashed. Aud was the one woman in this list.

From family names and other evidences it has been estimated that 84 per cent of the ancestors of the Icelanders came from Norway, 3 per cent from Sweden, and 12½ per cent from the British Isles, probably more from Ireland than Great Britain. The average stature of the Icelanders was slightly taller than that of the people in Scandinavia.

There was severe selection among those who fished in small boats off the coast of Iceland. Only the most vigorous, alert, and nimble survived, those individuals of greatest physical and mental efficiency.

In the hearts of the settlers who took land in Iceland, there was a deep desire for self-rule. This was accomplished through a lawthing in each of the thirteen districts into which they had divided the island. In 930 the people felt the need of unity under one authority which would promulgate laws for all districts. They formed an all-inclusive lawthing called the Althing, which was in essence a national parliament. The site chosen for the Althing was at Ixara, or Axe River, about twenty-three miles northeast of Reykjavik, and it was described in *Landnamabok:*

By a freak of nature an irregular oval mass about two hundred feet by fifty feet was left almost entirely surrounded by a crevice so deep and broad as to be utterly impassable; at one extremity alone a scanty causeway connected it with the adjoining level and allowed of access. Armed guards defended the entrance while the bondes [landowners] deliberated within. At the upper end, were three hummocks where sat chiefs and judges.

This site came to be called Thingveillir. Nearby was a drowning-pool in which witches were executed.

Being free from oppression and enjoying self-rule, Icelanders developed more of the characteristics of free men than any other folk of their time. Though King Harald wanted to rule Iceland, his power did not reach that far. The Icelanders built their own civilization and established an independent republic. This lasted until the second half of the thirteenth century, when the church and royal authority got control.

To this republic of enterprising men came the father of one of the world's great explorers and colonizers, Erik the Red.

5

Erik the Red

Erik the Red, a descendant of the kings of Rogaland and Agder in southwestern Norway and of a distinguished line of vikings, grew up in a bare, windswept region of Iceland. His father Thorvald Osvaldsson, who had been exiled from Norway "for the sake of manslaughters," settled on the peninsula north of Isafjörd at Hornstrands. All the agricultural land in Iceland had been homesteaded during the first fifty years of the settlement, but land of possible use as home bases for fishermen remained. Thorvald built a turf house near Drangar and ventured out among the drift ice, fishing. Erik spent his days on these dangerous waters, casting nets or spearing fish and seals, fighting walruses amid the ice floes.

In time Erik married. He chose as his wife a distant cousin, Thorhilda (Thjodhild), daughter of Jorund, son of Atli. Longing to find a better home for himself and his wife, Erik left the north and got possession of some fertile land among his wife's people in Haukadale. Once he cleared his land of rocks, he made his home, Erikstead, near Vatnshorn, a mountain on the north side of Haukadale. By his energy, grit, and shrewd bargaining, Erik had improved his status; he not only held a place among the well-established landowners but also he quarreled with them as an equal. The thralls of Erik, no doubt at their master's bidding, "let fall a rock slip upon the dwelling of Valthjof," which seems to have buried both house and occupant. Since rock slips were frequent in earthquake country, Erik may have hoped that the wrath of the gods would be accepted as the cause of Valthjof's demise. But considering the kind of man he was, Erik probably boasted of his successful imitation of the action of the gods. The mundane cause of the rock slip was in this case understood, and a feud began. Eyjolf the Foul (Saur), a kinsman of the rock-slip victim, slew Erik's men. "For that sake Erik slew Eyjolf, and also Island-Dueller (*Holmgang*) Hrafn." Thus the red-haired and hotheaded Erik in Iceland repeated his father's behavior in Norway. Eyjolf's kinsmen brought suit against Erik at the local lawthing for troublemaking and manslaughter. Erik was duly sentenced to banishment from Haukadale—a sentence that deprived him of his homestead as effectively as any rock slip.

Before leaving, he entrusted his deceased father's carved high-seat beams and the headposts of his sleeping platform to a man named Thorgest, who was to take good care of the precious heirlooms until Erik had built a new homestead. Erik spent the winter on two islands at the mouth of Hvammsfirth.

When his new homestead was ready, Erik asked for his high-seat posts and bedboards. Thorgest very unwisely refused to return them. With righteous indignation, Erik raided Thorgest's house and forcibly removed the valued pieces. Thorgest most foolishly pursued and fought with Erik. In the fray "two of Thorgest's sons fell, and some other men besides. Thereupon both sides sat at home amidst an armed company," hoping no doubt for a battle to the death.

That summer (probably 981) at the Thorsness lawthing, the case of Thorgest versus Erik the Red was adjudged. Since Erik had killed Thorgest's sons in a fair fight, he was sentenced only to lesser banishment from Iceland. This was a minor penalty, since it meant exile for only three years.

Erik placed his wife and children in the safe hands of close friends or kinsfolk. But where should he himself go? He went into hiding and thought it out. He recalled his father's telling him of Gunnbjörn Olfsson, a cousin who with Erik had the same greatgrandfather. This Gunnbjörn was said

to have been storm-driven a considerable distance west of
Iceland where he had discovered some skerries (isolated rocks
in the sea). However, no one had been able to find those
skerries again. Erik decided that, wherever they were, he
would spend the term of his exile there. He made careful
preparations, putting into his ship everything needed for years
in an uninhabited region. Thorgest's relatives and friends were
searching for him so assiduously that he was forced to stay in
hiding while his own friends readied his ship.

When the time came for departure, some of his friends
went with him as far as Snaefellsjökull, whose lofty peak rises
near the end of the promontory on the south side of Breidifjörd. This was the natural point of departure for anyone sailing westward. At parting, Erik revealed his plan and told his
friends that he and his crew would return in three years. Erik
prayed for Thor's guidance and protection and in the year
982 he steered his ship into the unknown.

Erik did not find Gunnbjörn's skerries, which may have
been reefs that disappeared as a result of volcanic action. The
reefs do not now exist.

The first land he sighted was a stretch of icy shore with a
gigantic glacier which he named Mid-Glacier. It is now called
Blacksark. Erik followed the land southward along icy wastes
and then, after rounding the southern tip of the land, turned
northward along its west coast. There he found fjords at
whose inner ends glaciers flowed down from an inland ice
field. But beneath the barren walls of the fjords lay ribbons
of grassland. This was a welcome surprise; certainly the prospect was far better than anything Erik had expected of Gunnbjörn's skerries. In fact, the fjords looked more inviting than
his boyhood home at Hornstrands.

Erik spent his first winter in the new country on what
was afterward called Eriksey (Erik's Island). This lay in a
wide inlet which Erik named Breidifjörd. In the spring he
explored the fjords that opened into Breidifjörd, drift ice pre-
venting his reaching the outer coast until summer. Near the
inner end of one fjord, which came to be known as Eriksfjörd

(now Tunugdliarfik), Erik found what seemed to him a favorable site for a permanent home. This was a slope which got maximum exposure to the sun. Erik must have thanked Thor for bringing him to a land where he would be the first homesteader with his choice of the land.

The *Landnamabok* does not say that he built his house at this time, but merely that "he took there a dwelling." This implies that he selected the land for his farmstead and set stone boundary markers. He may also have laid the foundations of his house so that he could later show that he had begun to build. It seems quite certain that he did not build that spring, for the *Landnamabok* tells us he spent the remaining two winters of his exile elsewhere. If he had built a house, he would probably have returned to it in the fall.

The first summer, as soon as departure of the drift ice permitted, he went, so the *Flateyjarbok* tells us, "into the western wastes and wide about here he assigned names to places." It is generally accepted that the "western wastes" comprised the coastal islands immediately west of Breidifjörd, where there are no habitable fjords, or the longer stretch of coast extending northwestward past the present Frederikshaab toward Godthaab. But they may have been the truly "western wastes" of Baffin Land. Erik "was the next winter at Eriksholmes (Erik's Islands) near Hvarfsgnipa," the turning peak or course-turning peak at Cape Farvel, the southern tip of Greenland. The *Landnamabok* says that the third summer "he went north as far as Scaefell, and came to Hrafnsfirth, and then he felt sure he had got around the extremity of Eriksfirth." The geography of the second winter and second summer is not clear. Eriksholmes was apparently not the island where he spent the first winter and the third one. There is no way of knowing which fjords he explored or what names he gave them. The one he called "Hrafnsfirth" did not retain that name, and all the fjords except Breidifjörd and Eriksfjörd got new names two or three years later.

The naming business, however, was central to the plan which Erik's later actions show must have been even then forming in his mind. He must have pictured to himself the advantages of persuading many other settlers to come to a country in which he had the best land in the most centrally located fjord. He obviously named headlands, islands, and fjords with a view to directing settlers to the best places, and he no doubt made charts and maps. Erik did not call the country "Glacier Land," though he foresaw that his men would describe the country as one with "very large glaciers," as indeed his men did when they returned to Iceland. He fetched around for a name that would take men's minds off the glaciers and that would make them dream of the interior fjords where they could raise cattle and have farmsteads. After all, the land had its drawbacks. Drift ice—as at Hornstrands— was a hindrance and a nuisance. Because of it, Erik could not get away the third spring. The *Landnamabok* says, pointedly, "Later in the summer he went to Iceland."

The name for the new land was inspired. "He called the land Greenland, for," the *Flateyjarbok* says, "he said that many men would desire to visit it if he gave the land a good name." This is what his contemporaries said he did. Much that cannot be substantiated has been written in the attempt to clear Erik from the charge of deliberately coining a mis- leading name. His defenders argue that Greenland must have been much greener then than now, that there must have been a great change of climate since Erik's day, and so on. Erik's admirers have even speculated about how many degrees warmer the land was a thousand years ago. Yet even if Green- land had been five degrees warmer, this would not have been enough for human beings to notice.

Aage Roussel [1] exonerates Erik completely:

There are no grounds whatsoever for regarding him as an agitator who, by not entirely straightforward propaganda (the attractive name "Greenland"), enticed his kinsmen from their

[1] "Farms and Churches in the Mediaeval Norse Settlements of Green- land," *Meddelelser om Grønland* (Copenhagen), Vol. 89, No. 1 (1941), pp. 6, 10.

homes into uncertainty. To a man like Erik, brought up in
the stern northland of Iceland, the luxuriant fjord banks of
Greenland must have seemed rich and promising.

Roussel goes on to give this undeniably accurate description:

*The southern point of Greenland is a wild and rugged
rocky landscape, just as barren as the east coast, which has
never contained possibilities for colonization by cattle breed-
ers. But as one travels up the west coast, the hospitality of the
country becomes warmer, commencing with Tasermuit Fjord,
and culminating at the northern part of Julianehaab Bay.*

Dr. Rhodes W. Fairbridge of Columbia University has
advanced strong evidence for the belief that the ocean level a
thousand years ago was somewhere between a half meter and
a meter higher than at present. I do not know of anyone who
has shown the ocean level was higher than this, and Fairbridge's evidence has not been successfully refuted. Let us
therefore assume that the ocean level was about 2½ feet
higher in Erik's day. Considering the areas of the oceans and
of the icecaps of Antarctica and Greenland, this would mean
that instead of 5,280 feet of thickness of icecap, Greenland
had an icecap only 5,230 feet thick. (The quantity of moisture
in a slightly warmer atmosphere would be comparatively in-
consequential.) Fifty feet less of ice in an icecap of such thickness would not change the predominant character of the land.
Then as now, an honest name for Greenland would have been
Whiteland. It was much more an ice-land than Iceland.

Some people have claimed that a thousand years ago the
climate was so much warmer that Greenland could not have
produced icebergs. Although the *Flateyjarbok* and *Hauksbok*
sagas do not mention icebergs, one cannot conclude that there
were none. The sagas do mention "glaciers." Why should
mariners, in giving others sailing directions, mention icebergs
which float here and there and are not in fixed locations? Can

there have been no icebergs off the Greenland coast in Erik's day in deference to the homesteaders?

The Greenland ice sheet is 1,600 miles long and up to 600 miles wide, and in places it extends beyond the coast. Annually 125 cubic miles of ice drop off into the sea, forming 10,000 to 15,000 large bergs. The East Greenland Current carries them into Davis Strait. Off Baffin Island, they are caught by the Labrador Current and carried southward. Most assuredly, the great outlet glaciers of Greenland were functioning in Erik's day.

The size and number of icebergs around Greenland and the southernmost latitude at which they appear differ from year to year. In 1964 the lanes of transatlantic shipping had to be shifted on account of an unusual invasion for this season. When a viking skipper approached an iceberg, he had sense enough to steer around it, and he would have no reason to tell folk at home of its temporary presence. There are hints in the sagas that almost all the viking voyages from and to Greenland occurred in summer or later, after the Greenland fjord mouths had been freed by the departure of pack ice. *The Floamanna Saga,* only portions of which have been translated into English,[2] says that Thorgils Örrabeinsstjup, stepson of Scarleg, was shipwrecked on the eastern coast of Greenland early in October. He and his men built a *skali* (long house) in which a partition separated two households. They "built a boat of driftwood and hides" in which they hoped to row away in the spring, but when May came, pack ice off shore prevented their escape. They "went up on a glacier but caught no glimpse of open sea." They could not get away all summer and had to spend another winter there. The second summer the departure of the pack ice permitted them to row away to the south. The summer after that they rounded the southern cape and luckily found a clear course "between the ice and the

[2] Translation by Sigrid Undset in "A Saga of Greenland," *Bulletin,* St. Ansgar's Scandinavian Catholic League of New York. No. 41 (February, 1943), pp. 1–14. Also a translation by Arth J. Tønnesen of Stavanger, Norway.

land until they came to Eriksfjörd." There they met a merchant ship whose owner was Thorstein the White, the closest friend of Thorgils. Thorstein gave Thorgils half his cargo. The two skippers sailed in the one ship to Brattahlid and wintered with their friend Erik the Red. "Erik was not very friendly or as hospitable as Thorgils had expected." We surmise that he was irked by the great popularity of Thorgils, whose sensational story of conquering adversity during his three-year adventure made him temporarily the most admired man in Greenland.

In naming Greenland, Erik the Red surely knew what he was doing and why. He knew what it was like to be envious of well-established farmsteaders. It might be argued that many land-hungry Icelanders would have emigrated to Greenland even if Erik had not acted like a real-estate promoter, and that his coining of the deceptive name merely speeded an inevitable process. In any event, as the glamorous word "Greenland" passed from lip to lip across Iceland, hundreds of persons decided to venture into the new country. They knew that however green the land was, they faced the task of establishing and maintaining themselves in a wilderness.

Meanwhile Erik resumed his personal feud with Thorgest. In whatever physical struggle there was, Erik this time was worsted, and so, as the *Landnamabok* says, "a reconciliation was effected between them." This was a blow to Erik's pride and probably hastened his determination to leave Iceland as soon as possible and forever. Other prospective colonists no doubt were driven by similar feelings. With Erik's leadership, there seems to have been ill-feeling from the beginning between Icelanders and the future Greenlanders. As a matter of fact, antipathies always existed between various viking settlements: vikings from Denmark, Sweden, or Norway raided the other countries; vikings in the Hebrides raided Norway; fishing rivals in the Shetlands and the Faeroes became at times almost enemies. History shows what a water passage of only twenty miles could do in allowing misunderstandings to arise between Normans in Normandy and Normans in England. The Icelanders who colonized Greenland

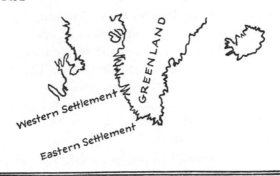

Eastern Settlement of Greenland

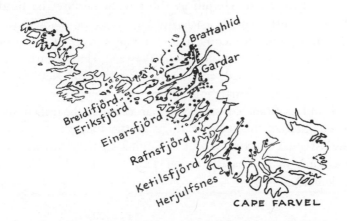

After choosing the best land for himself, Erik went home to Iceland and started back with twenty-five shiploads of immigrants. Only 14, however, reached Greenland. Erik named each fjord for the leader who first settled it. While most farmsteads, marked by dots on the map, were in the Eastern Settlement, Erik sent several ships up the coast to open the Western Settlement.

began at once to feel they were a different people from stay-at-home Icelanders.

In the early midsummer of 986, more than a thousand hardy pioneers crowded themselves into twenty-five ships, and set sail with Erik the Red for his well-advertised green country. Each hull was jammed with household effects, and horses, cattle, sheep, chickens, geese, pigs, goats, and dogs.

Only fourteen ships reached Greenland. The other eleven were lost at sea, driven back by head winds, or perhaps south to unreported landings. Five or six hundred persons arrived safely. Erik assigned each ship to one of eleven different fjords, including his own.

Each fjord was named for the leader of the shipload that first took land in it. The southernmost of the fjords thus settled, only about twenty-five miles north of Cape Farvel, was named for Herjulf, a grandson of a friend of Ingolf the Settler, "a most noble man, and a man held in the highest regard." Erik chose Herjulf as the one to occupy the fjord future colonists would reach first. Perhaps he wanted the only man prominent enough to become a rival to settle in the fjord farthest from his own. Between Herjulfsfirth and Eriksfjörd, the settled and named fjords were Ketilsfjörd, Hrafnsfjörd, and Einarsfjörd. These five along with Breidifjörd and Isafjörd, constituted what came to be called the Eastern Settlement. Two or three of the fourteen shiploads were assigned to fjords about 250 miles to the northwest of Eriksfjörd, in a separate region that became the Western Settlement.

6

Sailing Directions

When Erik the Red returned from the three years of exile, his first sighting of Iceland was what he had seen last when he sailed away, the summit of Snaefellsjökull on Snaefellsness. He steered toward it, for the *Landnamabok* says "he came to Breidifjörd." He brought to Icelanders more than news of a huge new land. He brought two pieces of information that were of great importance to viking navigators: the direction in which ships should sail from Snaefellsness to reach the southern tip of Greenland (the reverse of his return voyage), and his estimate of the distance of that sailing across open water out of sight of land.

From Erik's account of his short outward passage from Snaefellsness northwestward to the wastes on the east coast of Greenland, the vikings of Iceland soon discovered the shortest crossing by way of Kolbein's Isle. With Erik's contributions added to previously established knowledge of routes and sailing directions between Iceland and other lands, we find in the *Landnamabok* the complete list of the principal sailing directions:

From Norway, out of Stad, it is 7 days' sailing west to Horn in eastern Iceland; from Snaefellsness, 4 days' sailing west to Greenland. If one sails from Bergen straight west to Hvarf [Cape Farvel] in Greenland, one must keep about 12 sea miles south of Iceland. From Reykjanes in southern Iceland, 5 days' main to Jolduhlaup in Ireland going south; from

Langanes, in northern Iceland, 4 days' main north to Svalbard [Spitsbergen] in Hafsbotu [frozen sea]; but one day's sail to the Wastes of Greenland from Kolbein's Isle in the north.

The sailing directions reveal much more than distances and speeds, for they show that the vikings not only ventured back and forth everywhere in the North Atlantic but acquired a thorough knowledge of the positions of islands and lands and the shortest routes between them. An analysis of the Icelandic sailing directions is essential to an appreciation of Erik the Red's contribution and also to an understanding of subsequent discoveries to the southwest of Greenland.

Consider the sailing directions in clockwise order around Iceland. Look first at the one to the south. From Reykjanes, the southern promontory of Iceland, to the north coast of Ireland was "5 days' main." The direct distance from shore to shore is 794 miles. On the promontory near the point of Reykjanes, 7 miles inland, is a snow-capped peak 1,250 feet in altitude. Allowing for the curvature of the earth's surface, this peak is visible for 46 miles to the horizon. By subtracting the 7 miles, we have 39 miles as the distance that the peak is visible off shore. Subtract the 39 from 794, and we have 755 miles as the 5 days' sailing distance across the "main" or open ocean to Ireland.

Snaefellsjökull, the great landmark for mariners on Snaefellsness, has an altitude of 4,720 feet, visible at sea for 91 miles. At Hvarf, Cape Farvel, the southern tip of Greenland, there is a hill with an altitude of 800 feet. This is visible for 36 miles. Subtracting 91 and 36 from 725 miles, which is the great-circle distance from Snaefellsjökull to Cape Farvel, we have 598 miles for "4 days' main" from Iceland to Greenland.

From the north shore of Iceland northwestward to the Wastes (heavily glaciered shores) of eastern Greenland, the shortest distance is about 235 miles. Kolbein's Isle, which is 65 miles north of Iceland, is 40 miles nearer Greenland than is the north-central Iceland coast. In Greenland, 14 miles inland, there is a peak (Riguy B. J.) with an altitude of 2,385 feet. This is visible for 62 miles, or 48 miles off shore. From 235 we subtract 40 and 48, and are left with 147 miles for a one day's sail.

The sailing directions from Langanes, the promontory at the northeast corner of Iceland, north to Svalbard suggest an error in our reckoning. The great-circle distance from the tip of Langanes to the nearest point of Spitsbergen is 966 geographical miles. About 19 miles south of the tip of Langanes there is a mountain with an elevation of 2,335 feet, visible for over 63 miles and hence visible for 44 miles north of the tip of Langanes. Near the southern end of Spitsbergen is Hornsund, a mountain 3,032 feet high, visible for more than 72 miles. Subtracting 44 and 72 from 966, we have left 850

Sailing directions included the number of days it took to cross a certain stretch of ocean before sighting land. The author's drawing here translates viking sailing days from Iceland into miles.

miles. Yet this appears to be the distance which the viking mariners said was "4 days' main." But trace on a globe the great-circle from Langanes to the southern tip of Spitsbergen, and you will see that the great-circle passes close to the eastern side of Jan Mayen Island, whose active volcano 7,608 feet in altitude is visible for 115 miles. The fiery summit of Jan Mayen was visible for 115 miles when approaching it and visible for 115 miles when leaving it astern. From 850 miles let us subtract 115 and 115, or 230 miles. This gives us 620 miles as the distance of "4 days' main." If we make allowance for mast-height visibility in approaching and leaving Jan Mayen Island, the 620 miles is reduced to 605.

This is conclusive proof that to the mind of the viking mariner the word "main" meant ocean out-of-sight of land— the main part of the ocean and not a portion recognizable in relation to some known and visible land.

Our data thus far are:

	Distance of "main" in miles	Number of days	One day's sailing distance
To Ireland	755	5	151
To tip of Greenland	598	4	149½
To Wastes of Greenland	147	1	147
To Spitsbergen	605	4	151½

A one-day (24-hour) sailing distance across open ocean with no land visible was 150 miles at slightly more than 5½ knots. This was sailing with a steady following wind. It was by no means the maximum speed possible. There are records of viking ships having made 8 to 10 or more knots under exceptional conditions. Sailing directions, however, were for the guidance of ships of average capacity under ordinary conditions.

Now turn to the sailing directions for the voyage between Stad in Norway and Höfn (Horn Harbor) in southeastern Iceland. The direct distance is 713 miles. But 45 miles west of

Winds and ocean currents affected sailing time. Shown above are some currents that helped and hindered viking explorers.

Höfn is snow-covered Oraefajökull, with an altitude of 6,950 feet, visible over the horizon for 110 miles, and hence visible for 65 miles to a mariner approaching Höfn from the east. The mast-height visibility was about 7½ miles at each end of the voyage, or a total of 15 miles. And hills near Stad were visible for about 30 miles. Subtract 65 and 15 and 30 miles from 713, and we see that 603 miles is the distance out of sight of land for what must have been originally stated not as "7" but as "4 days' sailing." The other data make it four to one that "7" was a copyist's error.

The customary viking sailing route between Stad and Horn was, however, not directly west by great circle. There was a good reason why not. Prevailing westerlies made such a route only rarely possible. East winds are relatively infrequent in that area and not likely to last more than a day or two at the most. When an east wind came, a mariner waiting at Stad would set his course due west to the Shetland Islands, only 215 miles away, less than a day and a half of sailing distance. He would probably stay in the port of Shetland for several days or weeks waiting for another favorable wind. If he came as a trader, he would wish to stay there for a considerable time. When the right wind came, he would sail north and west away from the Shetlands. His passage over the main to the Faeroes would again require less than a day and a half of sailing.

Finally, from the Faeroes to Horn in Iceland he had to sail 322 miles. This meant that he had to sail about 232 miles out of sight of land. He approached Horn from the southeast, where the peak of Oraefajökull was first visible about 90 miles away. This last leg of the mariner's voyage from Stad to Horn via the Shetlands and Faeroes was 75 to 100 miles longer than the direct great-circle route, but it was almost precisely the same distance out of sight of land.

What a mariner wished to know from others who had preceded him on a course was the distance across the main. How long a time he might choose to spend in any port en route was his own business. The over-all time a ship might take between Stad and Horn via the Shetlands and Faeroes might be, and usually was, several weeks. But these were not ordinarily spent wallowing around fighting head winds.

The long-distance passage "from Bergen straight west to Hvarf in Greenland" was feasible only if favorable nonwesterly winds continued. A great circle from Stad to the southern tip of Greenland passes through the Faeroes. If a mariner ventured the 400 miles directly from Stad to the Faeroes instead of island hopping via the Shetlands, he could put into port in the Faeroes if the winds were adverse. In any case, in pur-

Viking marauders shattered the peace of the Irish monks who lived their lives of devotion and privation in beehive-shaped cells like this one on Skellig Michael, a rocky island off the Kerry coast. A shrine visited by crowds of pilgrims who no doubt left behind mementos, it was raided in 823.

When the Danes captured East Anglia in 870, King Edmund refused to renounce his Christian faith in favor of a pagan religion. Therefore, the legend says, he was tied to a tree and killed by arrows. This ninth-century manuscript illumination shows three Danes leading Edmund to his death, while two others drive him on with maces.

The Royal Library, Copenhagen

Here is a page of the *Flateyjarbok*, a fourteenth-century collection of sagas recounting the exploits of viking explorers.

Norwegian Information Service

Scandinavian vikings got their name from the viks, or fjords, from which they sailed in search of wealth and adventure. Many came from farms perched on the slopes of fjords.

The warlike Norsemen used
ship figureheads like this
one to terrify their victims
when invading inland wa-
ters.

Reconstructed viking barracks at Trelleborg, Sweden. It could
house a hundred warriors.

Pictures were carved on rocks in Norway and Sweden many centuries before the viking era. This carving of a skin-boat was photographed near Stockholm.

Three ships of viking times have been found well preserved. One, the warship shown here, was unearthed at Oseberg, Norway, in 1904.

A fourth-century boat discovered at Nydam, Denmark, carries oars and a rudder but no sails. Peabody Museum's model is shown here.

This photograph shows the Oseberg ship, in the ship museum in Oslo, Norway, as it looks now after restoration. In it archaeologists found everything useful, from a pair of scissors to three richly carved sleighs.

Norse runemasters carved inscriptions on weapons and gravestones to charm away evil. This stone from Västergötland, Sweden, has runes on one side and pictures on the other.

Detail from an eighth-century Gotland stone showing Odin, Norse god of victory, mounted on a charging horse. Prisoners taken in battle were often sacrificed to him.

suing the passage "straight west" to Greenland, he had to pass through the Faeroes or clear their northern end; and from off their northern end, the great circle to the southern tip of Greenland passes within twenty miles of the southernmost coast of Iceland. The sailing direction, "keep about 12 sea miles south of Iceland," shows how knowledgeable the vikings were.

7

Bjarni Herjulfsson

It was with sailing directions like these that a young viking trader made his way to Greenland. Along the way, though exploration was not his intent, he discovered three new lands to the west. Because his voyage forms so important a link in the history of viking exploration, I have translated and give here the entire narrative from the *Flateyjarbok*.

Bjarni, the son of an Icelander named Herjulf, had in his youth an inclination for voyaging and a shrewd eye for trade, so that he prospered and won the respect of his fellows. He became the owner of a trading ship and made it his custom to sail abroad one year and to return the next, in order to spend every other winter at home with his father in Iceland.

One season, before Bjarni returned, his father decided to go with Erik the Red as a colonist to Greenland. Herjulf settled on a cape near the southern end of Greenland, and was the leading man of the region. In the summer of the same year [986], Bjarni arrived at Eyrar in Iceland and was much surprised to hear of the move which his father had made. Bjarni would not unload his cargo, and when his shipmates asked what he intended to do, he replied that it was his purpose to keep to his custom and to spend the winter with his father.

"I will take the ship to Greenland if you will go with me."

They all replied that they would follow him wherever he decided to go. Then Bjarni said: "Our voyage into the Greenland Sea must be regarded as foolhardy, since none of us has ever been there."

Nevertheless they put to sea when they had provisioned their ship; and after three days' sail when the land was hidden by the water, the fair wind failed and changed into north winds and fogs, and they knew not where they were carried, and this uncertainty lasted many days. When the sun came forth again, they were able to establish direction from the heavens, and they hoisted sail and sailed for a day before they sighted land. They wondered what land it could be. Bjarni doubted if it were Greenland. Bjarni's shipmates asked whether he wished to sail to the land, but he proposed that they merely sail close to it, and as they did so, they soon perceived that the land was mountainless and wooded with low hillocks.

Leaving the land on their larboard with their sail swung over toward it, they sailed for two days before they sighted another land. They asked Bjarni whether he thought this was Greenland, but he said this was no more like Greenland than the first, because he had been told that in Greenland there were mountains with very large glaciers. When they drew near this land, they saw it was flat and extensively wooded.

The fair wind then failed, and the crew thought it prudent to land, but Bjarni refused. The men pretended that they needed wood and water, to which Bjarni replied: "You have no lack of either," and for this assertion he brought criticism upon himself from his shipmates.

They hoisted sail when he bade them to, and turning the prow from the land they sailed out upon the high seas, with gales from the southwest, and after three days' sailing saw a third land which was high and mountainous with glaciers. When Bjarni was asked whether he wished to land, he said he did not, because this land seemed unprofitable. Without lowering their sail, they coasted along this land and perceived it was an island.

They left this land astern, and sailed on with the same fair wind. The wind rose mightily and Bjarni commanded them to reef, to slacken speed for the sake of the ship and rigging. They now sailed for four days. Then they saw a fourth land, and this time Bjarni said: "This is most like Greenland, *according to my information, and here we may steer to the land."* This they did, and came to land in the evening, below a cape at which there was a boat, and upon this cape dwelt Bjarni's father, Herjulf, for whom the cape was named Herjulfsness. Bjarni now joined his father, and gave up voyaging and remained with his father as long as Herjulf lived, and made his home there after his father died.

This is all we know of Bjarni's voyage. His custom of spending one winter "abroad" and the next winter in his father's home grew out of necessity. Although only a few days of sailing were needed for the passage between Iceland and Norway, a single sailing season was not long enough for a round trip by a busy trader. The season was usually from May to the end of September or the first part of October. Bjarni had to spend much time waiting for favorable winds. And no doubt he liked to visit friends in each port. Certainly he had commissions for various customers and needed time to exchange goods in his ship for the return voyage. In Iceland, Bjarni picked up such goods as furs, skins, fish, ivory, wool, and tallow. He exchanged these things in Norway for metal tools and weapons, grain, jewelry, and building timber needed for doorframes and for ship repairs. The timber especially fetched high prices in Iceland.

As it happened, Bjarni sailed abroad the odd-numbered years. On the important voyage in question he returned to Iceland sometime in August, 986—the year in which Erik the Red led the first settlers to Greenland.

Anticipating the usual reception in Iceland, he was disappointed by his father's failure to appear. But knowing his father's readiness to seize opportunity, Bjarni was probably not much surprised to learn that his father had sailed with Erik to establish a new farmstead on broad green meadows in some sheltered fjord in a new country.

Many folk came to Bjarni's ship eager to buy or trade for the goods he had brought from abroad but Bjarni "would not unload his cargo." He astutely sensed that he could trade more profitably in Greenland, because everything in his ship would be in great demand in an entirely new country. When Bjarni asked how to reach Greenland, he was given the sailing directions and the distinguishing feature reported by the men who had been with Erik the Red: "mountains with very large glaciers." He learned also that it had many islands and reefs along its western coast. As an experienced mariner, Bjarni gave fair warning to his shipmates when they said they would go with him to Greenland: "Our voyage into the Greenland Sea must be regarded as foolhardy, since none of us has ever been there."

Nothing daunted, they put aboard food and fresh water and raised sail. In departing, Bjarni had to sail in three directions and for 300 to 400 miles before he lost sight of Iceland. First, he had to skirt the south coast westward from Eyrar to turn Cape Reykjanes. Then he had to sail northward until he had the summit of Snaefellsjökull to the northeast of him, in the opposite direction to what Erik the Red had given as the direction for the direct crossing from Snaefellsjökull to Hvarf. Not until then could Bjarni set his course southwestward from Snaefellsjökull with confidence that he would be headed toward the southern tip of Greenland.

After Snaefellsjökull fell below the horizon, the east wind failed and north winds blew them southward into fog banks and they were lost for many days, at least fifteen to twenty days. The Labrador Current carried them a very great distance to the south and west. When they saw the sun again, Bjarni perceived from the noon shadows that he was far south of Iceland and therefore far south of Greenland. He sailed for a day, probably northward or northwestward, before he sighted land ahead. When they drew close they saw that it was "wooded with low hillocks." However, because it was late in the sailing season, Bjarni knew it was advisable to reach Greenland as soon as possible. He therefore did not go ashore, but turned his prow to the northeast, away from the land. That land did not permit of further westward sailing and he knew Greenland was somewhere to the north.

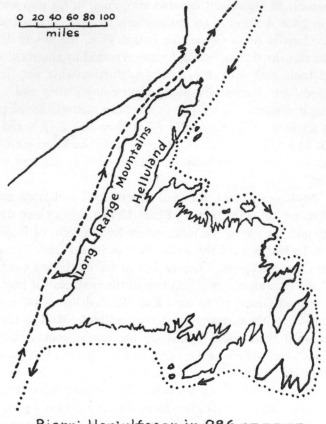

O 20 40 60 80 100
miles

Bjarni Herjulfsson in 986 ------
Leif Erikson in 1003 ·················

On his way to Greenland, Bjarni Herjulfsson was carried by the Labrador Current southward past Newfoundland. Seventeen years later Leif Erikson, with Bjarni's ship and some of his crew, made a voyage still farther down the coast of North America.

He sailed for two days before he sighted another land. This he saw as "flat and extensively wooded." This is a perfect description of the southern coast of Nova Scotia near Halifax, which looks extraordinarily flat, since the hills in that country lie too far inland to be visible from off the southern shore. Without mountains or glaciers, this second land also could not be Greenland. Being aware of the need for hurry, Bjarni refused to go ashore but took advantage of "gales from the southwest," which means he continued to sail to the northeast.

"After three days' sailing" he "saw a third land which was high and mountainous with glaciers." In summer a stationary cloud visible for eighty miles always hangs over a snow field on a mountain close to the southwest corner of a great island northeast of Nova Scotia. If Bjarni saw this cloud low above the horizon, he knew that it indicated land and would have steered toward it. When he came near enough to sight the land, the snow field and others that looked like glaciers made Bjarni think for a little while that it might be Greenland. Having been told that the destination of Erik the Red and his colonists had been the fjords on the western side of Greenland, Bjarni sailed northward along the western side of this third land. From the absence of ocean swells off its west coast, he knew the land was between him and the ocean. "They coasted along this land and perceived it was an island." If it had been a small island, the saga would not have used the revealing words "coasted along." The coast was long. One cannot perceive that a large land is an island merely by sailing in the offing along one side of it, but only by circumnavigating it. When Bjarni finally cleared the island's north end and came out into the open ocean again, he realized that during his fogbound voyage from Iceland he had simply not sighted its eastern side.

It was a huge island, and we know what island it was. The last portion of Bjarni's voyage tells us in what direction and at what distance from the southern tip of Greenland the great island's northern end lay. It was Newfoundland. We know that Bjarni coasted its western side not only from choice but because only along that western side are there mountains whose valleys even in the summer retain snow fields that look like glaciers.

The passage out of sight of land from the northern tip of

Newfoundland to the southern tip of Greenland starts from where one leaves Belle Isle astern and out of sight. It ends with the sighting of a snow peak in southern Greenland. The 660-foot elevation on Belle Isle is visible at sea at mast height for 40 miles, and a mountain of 4,900-foot elevation near Herjulfsness is visible at sea at mast height for 90 miles. By subtracting 40 and 90 from the land-to-land distance of 698, we have 568 miles out of sight of land for four days' sailing under reefed sail in rough seas with "a wind that rose mightily."

From his first land to his second, and from there to the third land, Bjarni sailed for 2 days plus 3 days. After he "left this land [Newfoundland] astern, and sailed on with the same fair wind," he "now sailed for four days." Then they saw a fourth land, and this time Bjarni said: "This is most like Greenland, according to my information, and here we may steer to the land."

The days mentioned in the saga story make the total distance from Bjarni's first land to Greenland 2 plus 3 plus 4, or only 9 days' sailing. But to those 9 days we must add also the hours it took Bjarni's ship after sighting the second and third lands to draw close to them and to leave them astern, and also there must be added the distance (and time) Bjarni sailed while he "coasted along" the third land. Bjarni must have coasted along Newfoundland for at least a day and a half. After Bjarni "left this land astern," he sailed for 4 days before he sighted Greenland. He came to shore in Greenland "in the evening." Thus, the final hours from dawn to evening must also be added. Bjarni's voyage from the first land he sighted to the southern tip of Greenland took something over 11 days, and it was more than 1,650 miles, almost 1,700 miles. His total nonstop voyage from Iceland to Greenland extended across 3,500 miles of ocean. The happy ending, his arriving that last evening at the mouth of the very fjord to which his father had been assigned, was a well-deserved reward for masterly navigation.

8

The Greenland Settlements

The first settlers in Greenland were amazingly fit. Though half the English settlers at Plymouth, Massachusetts, died their first winter, there is no record that any of the Greenland settlers, though five times more numerous, died in their first winter of 986/7. The Greenlanders had been raised in Iceland, where sickly infants were exposed and severe conditions weeded out weaklings. A man who settled with Erik in Eriksfjörd was "Thorkell, nephew of Erik and of exceeding strength. He swam out to Hvalsey [Whale Island] after an old ox, and brought it from the island on his back, when he wanted to give good cheer to his kinsman, Erik, and there was not a seaworthy vessel at hand. That was a distance of half a sea mile." In near-freezing waters! The incident seems almost incredible, but cattle in those times, before recent centuries of selective breeding, had only two thirds the length and one third the weight of cattle today. Even so, Thorkell's feat gives insight into the physical stamina of Erik's colonists.

These settlers were not the first people to live among the Greenland fjords. The *Islendingabok* says: "Both east and west in the country they found human habitations, fragments of skin boats and stone implements from which it was evident that the same kind of people had been there as inhabited Vinland and whom the Greenlanders called Skraelings [Shriekers, War-Whoopers]." The vikings do not seem to have discriminated between Eskimos and Indians. The Eskimos were nomadic hunters who had moved away but would someday return.

By natural increase and by influx of new settlers, the first colony in the New World grew quickly. Before the end of the eleventh century there were 90 farmsteads in the Western Settlement and 190 in the principal or Eastern Settlement. Most of the houses were on slopes above the shores of the fjords, each house located where it had the the best available view. The great majority of farmsteads were ten to twenty or more miles in from the seacoast. The Greenland colony attained a population of over three thousand, pressing the country's food resources to the limit. The Greenlanders ate fish, meat, and dairy products, but little else. On the most sheltered meadows there may have been attempts at first to grow rye, oats, and barley, but the crops were too thin to justify the effort. Some colonists managed to raise a few cabbages and onions in favored spots. Other vegetables were unobtainable. The only wheat or other grain the colonists ever saw were small quantities brought from Europe in trading ships. Cattle fed only on grass. Fish and meat were preserved by drying, smoking, and freezing.

Erik's farmstead, which he called Brattahlid, had the best location in Greenland. It extended for 2,000 feet along the shore of his fjord and, at its widest from shore to mountain wall, for about one quarter of a mile. In addition, upland pastures extended to the west of the ridge. The excellence of this land for cattle grazing seems to have been Erik's primary consideration in selecting the area. A narrow but rather deep river ran down near the north end of his land, and the salmon fishing in that river was the best in the whole country. Erik had cow barns on his land with a total number of stalls for thirty cows, and each barn had its own covered haystack.

In the permafrost or near to permafrost soil of Greenland the foundations of buildings and some of the timbers and utensils have been surprisingly well preserved, as extensive archaeological investigations have revealed. This is why Dr. Johannes Brøndsted, director of the National Museum in Copenhagen, says: "It is odd that most of our knowledge about Nordic houses in viking times and the Middle Ages should be derived from distant Greenland."

Erik had several good reasons in selecting for his dwelling a location north of the river. The site was on a slope near the shore, with excellent drainage possibilities. This meant that he could have an abundant supply of water in the center of his

Erik the Red lived with his wife Thorhilda and three sons in a farmstead named Brattahlid, which stood high above the fjord. His land was excellent for cattle grazing, and the river running through it was full of salmon. Remains of his houses and barns, diagramed here, have been found by archaeologists.

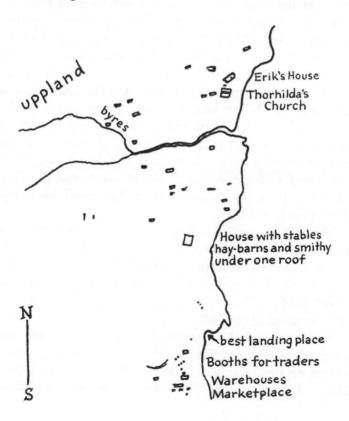

uppland

byres

Erik's House

Thorhilda's Church

House with stables hay-barns and smithy under one roof

N

S

best landing place

Booths for traders

Warehouses

Marketplace

house. He laid one conduit to bring surface water into a cistern and another under the opposite wall to carry off the excess. The interior cistern provided a means for extinguishing any fire started by accident or by enemies. The entrance to the house was less than fifty feet from a natural out-of-doors well for drinking water that flowed without freezing all winter. This outdoor well has "no counterpart in Greenland," says the archaeologist who examined it.

Erik's dwelling was a "long house," or hall, with interior dimensions of about 48 feet by 15 feet. It was essentially a sod-walled room, except that on the inside its walls were faced with some stones held together with turf. On the outside there was a protecting wall of turf, so that the total thickness of the walls was about eight feet. The stones themselves were flat fieldstones from the vicinity; in structures built later, the proportion of smaller blocks and round boulders increased, because the choice blocks had been used up. The floor of the hall was well-tamped gravel with slabs of stone laid over it. The roof was turf laid on poles that rested on posts inside the walls.

There were several fireplaces. One near the south end was eight feet long. There were fireplaces in the center of the hall to keep the water in the cistern and conduits from freezing. Close to the west wall, opposite the entrance, was a fireplace for cooking, with a rectangular shallow pit and raised slabs around it. Some unburned bits of wood amid the charcoal debris from the fireplaces show that dwarf birch and willow grew in the area.

The hall was used as a living room and upon occasion as a festive hall for banqueting. It housed looms for spinsters. If there was originally a sleeping platform along one side, it was removed when Erik erected a more serviceable house for himself and family with sleeping rooms at the later dwelling site to the northeast of the hall.

As in many of the Greenland houses, Erik's family ate their meals seated on chairs around a table. It was the custom in those days to have tablecloths. On the table were knives, plates, and spoons fashioned out of wood or soapstone. There was a family devotion at each meal—in Erik's house a prayer to Thor. The folk were cleanly. They offered a towel to a guest. Women heated water to wash wounds, and they used cow urine (ammonia) for washing clothes.

Since Erik's hall was windowless, he placed it so that its doorway commanded the best view down the fjord. In this respect it resembled the houses of vikings everywhere. This placement was probably not arranged for admiring the scenery but for keeping an eye on the cattle, and guarding against an enemy approaching by water. The *Floamanna Saga* tells us that while friends of Erik's, Thorgils and Thorstein, with their men, were guests at Brattahlid, some vikings won a foothold on an island off Eriksfjörd, and from their stronghold harassed the settlements. Thorgils and Thorstein descended on them, and took their two ships, *Stakanhöfdi* and *Vinganaut*. It seems likely that these names mean "Squally Headland" and "Wine Frenzy."

Brattahlid had spacious outhouses for many men, and for an entire winter Erik entertained eighty unexpected visitors. In the area just south of the river there was later a sprawling structure with sleeping rooms, stables, hay barns, and smithy all under one roof, where the occupants could hole up during heavy winter snows without needing to go out. There was a similar combined dwelling, stable, barn, and smithy near the south end of the Brattahlid land. At the middle of Erik's land, just south of the best landing place, there were booths for traders, a market place, and warehouses. The largest warehouse was 65 feet by 25 feet inside. Erik let Thorgils and Thorstein store their shipload of merchandise "in one of his warehouses." This market place area was undoubtedly where the Greenland Althing met for the first century.

Near the landing place was a "boat hollow" of ship form where walls of stones and turf protected Erik's ship when drawn ashore for the winter. Some covering must have been laid across the walls to keep snow and ice out of the interior of the open ship.

Before leaving Erik's farmstead, one other detail should

be mentioned which has pertinent bearing on our story. Archaeologists have found on Erik's farm the bones of a horse which show that the animal was no more than six and one-half feet long, with a shoulder height of only fifty inches. In viking times horses in Iceland and Greenland were the size of what we today call ponies. Note the comparative size of horse and rider in the carving on the Stone from Möjebro in Hagby Socken, Uppland, Sweden.

Erik lived at Brattahlid with his wife and three sons: Leif, Thorvald, and Thorstein. He had a natural daughter, Freydis, of whom the *Flateyjarbok* says: "She was called Erik's daughter; she was wedded to a man called Thorvard. She was very proud, but Thorvard was a little man; she was chiefly given to him for his wealth's sake." Freydis and her husband resided in another fjord. Erik's wife Thorhilda may have expressed her disapproval of Erik's having fathered Freydis, and Erik's sons probably heard much talk of her.

Erik prospered. However, a few years after the colony started, it was obvious that for most of the settlers life was becoming more difficult. There was no more wood after all the driftwood and the few stunted birches and willows had been used. The general economy was dependent on trade. As leading man in the settlements, Erik had first choice of the trade goods brought into his fjord. For most of the colonists there was a very real problem of how to get enough trading ships to come to Greenland. Lacking timber, they could not build ships for themselves. What the Greenlanders had to offer in trade were furs, sealskins, bearskins, ropes made from walrus hide, walrus-teeth ivory, eider-duck feathers, tallow from beef and mutton fat, some hunting falcons, on rare occasions a polar bear cub,[1] and any quantity of steatite or

---

[1] I am indebted to Arth J. Tønnesen of Stavanger, Norway, for a translation of the *Saga of Audun Vestfirdling*. According to this saga, Audun got hold of a tame white bear in Greenland and took it to King Sven of Denmark, who treated him handsomely. As payment for the bear, Sven gave Audun a fine trading ship, with the best farm produce for its cargo, and a bag of silver money, and an armband of gold. Think of it, one animal worth more than an ocean-going ship!

soapstone plates, bowls, spoons, and other handmade utensils. Of all these goods, the only ones not available to the European market in larger quantity and at less distance in Iceland were the soapstone articles, the falcons, and polar bear furs and cubs. In their desperate efforts to compete with Icelandic traders, Greenlanders had the odds stacked against them. Erik the Red must have seen with dismay how his country was failing to meet the challenge.

9

Leif Erikson's Education

Erik's son Leif had memories of his boyhood in Iceland. Grown to manhood, thirteen years after the Greenland Colony had started, he was restless and eager for adventure. When he expressed his desire to see other countries, Erik was glad to let him go. In particular, Erik hoped that Leif could explain the economic situation to the king of Norway and that the king would assign more ships to the trade with Greenland. There was some basis for these hopes, for several of Erik's relatives had married relatives of the king. And the king had recently laid the foundations of the merchant town of Nidaros (called Trondhjem for several centuries, but now Trondheim) because of his interest in trade. Leif would be his father's ambassador.

Erik therefore provided a ship and men, and Leif prepared to sail as early in the summer of 999 as the departure of drift ice from the mouth of the fjord permitted. When the time came, Erik invoked the blessing of the gods on his son's voyage. Leif embraced his parents and brothers, and they gave each other into Thor's keeping.

Leif sailed from Eriksfjörd, and clearing the southern end of Greenland, set his prow eastward. He came to land 1,500 miles away in the Hebrides. Perhaps he had been driven off course by storms, as some writers have suggested. More probably he landed in the Hebrides intentionally. They lay at the crossroads of trade in and out of the Irish Sea and between Ireland and Norway. He may have tried to interest shipowners in trade with Greenland.

The Hebrides had been discovered in viking times by one of Leif's distant cousins, Ketil Flatnose, whose son became king of the Norse in Dublin, and whose grandson became king of the Norse in Scotland. There were men in the Hebrides who had met Erik the Red, and everyone had heard of him. His handsome son Leif was well received.

Whatever Leif may have said in the Hebrides about trade with Greenland, we know the kind of thing he was soon saying on another subject. He met a girl. The *Saga of Erik the Red* calls her a woman of good family. She had a good heathen name, Thorgunna, and she is described in words that show the viking genius for expression—a whole novel in a phrase—a woman "who knew more than a little."

There was much she knew better than Leif, but she was a capable teacher and he was more than tractable. He stayed on through all that summer, enjoying the education. When any of her watchful family suggested that he should sail for Norway, he had only to point to the sky and say that the wind did not seem to be in the right direction. Under Thorgunna's tutelage it was easy for a young man to be a bit confused about wind directions. It is hard to believe that the weather conspired with Frey, or that the west wind, prevailing in other summers, refused to blow at all that summer. If we had meteorological records as far back as 999, we would check on Leif's excuse. But then we do know the direction of the wind that season. Wherever Thorgunna was, it blew toward her.

Leif's men observed the atmospheric conditions that enveloped their young leader and they were considerably entertained thereby. When at last in the autumn the wind began to blow away from Thorgunna and Leif prepared to leave, Thorgunna asked him to take her with him. This brought to the young man a new problem as sticky as trade. There were her relatives to consider. They knew their kinswoman was chiefly responsible and they did not blame the youth from Greenland for what had happened, but Leif saw that if he took her away with him, they could accuse him of woman stealing. A chip off the old block, he shrewdly asked Thorgunna if her kinsfolk would assent to her being carried away, and she didn't help because she said she couldn't care less what their attitude might be. And then romance dissolved into reality.

His men who remembered the story preserved (in the *Flateyjarbok*) some of the conversation between Leif and Thorgunna, words uttered in a scene before witnesses, probably as the ship was about to depart. Leif told Thorgunna he would not risk taking her with him, "and we so few in numbers."

"You may find you are making a mistake," Thorgunna argued.

Leif replied: "I shall put it to the proof notwithstanding."

"Then you shall hear it," said Thorgunna. "I no longer have only myself to consider; for I am pregnant, and the responsibility is yours. I foresee that I shall give birth to a male child. Even though you abandon me, I shall rear the boy. [She would not expose him as an unwanted child.] I shall send him to you in Greenland, when he is able to take his place among men. It is my guess you will get as much profit of this son as you deserve from this our parting. Furthermore, I intend to come to Greenland myself before I die."

Troubled by Thorgunna's words and sorry for her, Leif proved he was as much of a gentleman as any heathen ever was. He gave her a finger ring of gold, tantamount to a public acknowledgment of an engagement, if not acknowledgment of her as his wife. He presented her with a wadmal mantle woven of wool from Greenland sheep, and as further evidence that he and she were bound together, he gave her a belt, probably his own belt, adorned, we may imagine, with much-prized walrus ivory. What more could he have done, short of settling in the Hebrides for the rest of his life? He had promised his father to go to Norway.

He sailed without Thorgunna. While he was in Norway

she gave birth to a son, as she had predicted, and named him Thorgils. Leif publicly acknowledged his paternity. Thorgunna took Thorgils to Iceland the next year. She died there, and Thorgils was then taken to Greenland.

Crossing from the Hebrides and sailing up the coast of Norway, Leif Erikson felt he would never again in all his life be so deeply moved. He could not foresee his reception in Nidaros.

Like all Norsemen, Leif had heard that after the death of King Harald, his son Hakon had made an attempt to introduce Christianity into Norway. Hakon talked the bondes into making him king by promising to give to every bonde the udal rights (ownership in fee simple to the land he lived on) and thus return what his father had taken from them. Snorre Sturlason in *The Heimskringla* (*A History of the Norse Kings*) says:

All men rejoiced at the news, and it passed from mouth to mouth—it flew, like fire in grass, through the whole land. . . . Since the whole country was heathen, Hakon practiced his Christianity in private.

When in 950 Hakon ventured to urge the bondes to allow themselves to be baptized, great was the murmur and noise among the crowd.

Asbjorn answered thus to the king's proposal: "We bondes, King Hakon, when we elected thee to be our king, and got back our udal rights, thought we had got into heaven; but now we don't know whether we have really got back our freedom." [King Hakon was flatly told some home truths, with a veiled threat.] "This is an extraordinary proposal—that we should abandon the ancient faith which our forefathers have held from the oldest times when the dead were burnt, as well as laid under mounds. . . . Thou, king, must use some moderation and only require from us such things as we can obey thee in."

The bondes gave loud applause to this speech. When silence was again restored, Earl Sigurd, who presided on behalf of the king at all festivals of sacrifice said: "It is King Hakon's will to give way to you." The bondes replied that it was their desire that the king should offer a sacrifice as his father was wont to do.

The king publicly drank ale in the name of Thor, by making over it the sign of his hammer (his fist?) before he drank it, but he would not eat the flesh of a horse that had been sacrificed to idols. Earl Sigurd persuaded the people not to lay hands on Hakon. He asked the king to hold his mouth over the handle of the kettle upon which the fat smoke of the boiled horse flesh had settled. The king laid clean linen over the handle and then held his nose over it. The people were not satisfied. The king was forced to take some bits of horse liver and to drain goblets without first making the sign of the cross.

King Hakon unwisely attacked the bondes, and bloodshed followed. In one desperate battle, warriors bared their naked breasts as a sign of courage and scorn. The king was slain. He was later called Hakon the Good. The new king had resolved to force the Christian religion upon Norway once and for all.

Leif's first impression of King Olaf Tryggvason, to use the words of *Heimskringla*, was that he was "the handsomest of men, very stout and strong, and in all bodily exercises, he excelled every Norseman that ever was heard of."

The *Heimskringla* story of Olaf Tryggvason is one of the most romantic in all history. His queen mother gave birth to him in 963 or 964 on an island in a lake, where she was hiding from enemies. She attempted to take the child to her brother King Valdemar in Russia. Her ship was captured by vikings in the eastern Baltic and the child was held in Eistland (Estonia) until he was nine. When the queen's nephew came to Eistland from Holmgard (Novgorod) on King Valdemar's business, he observed a handsome boy in the market place. When the boy explained who he was, he was taken to his cousin's house in Holmgard. "There one day he saw a man who had killed his foster father, and with his small ax he clove the man's skull to the brain. In Holmgard it was the law to slay whoever puts a man to death except by judgment of law, and the whole people stormed and sought after the boy." The wife of King Valdemar said the boy appeared too comely to allow him to be slain, and she paid a fine to save him. King Valdemar received Olaf into his court, where he stayed until he was seventeen. Then he was made chief of the men-at-arms, and when he went warring, he was victorious everywhere. At twenty he went plundering in Friesland, Saxonland, and Flaemingjaland, and finally he joined a four-year expedition to Northumbria in England, to Scotland, the Hebrides, the Isle of Man, and Ireland. In Ireland he married Gyda, daughter of an Irish king, after slaying a disappointed rival in single combat. In 991 he came with ninety-three ships to Folkestone, Sandwich, and Ipswich; after the Battle of Maldon the English paid him £10,000 in tribute. Three years later he and Sweyn attacked London and were bought off with £16,000. A persuasive holy man, however, converted him to Christianity and Olaf promised he would never return to England in hostility. From Dublin he sailed to the Hebrides and Orkneys. He threatened the earl of Orkney with fire and sword if he and his people did not accept Christianity. The earl chose the easy way to peace.

In 995 Olaf landed in Norway and the next year was elected king. He declared he would bring all Norway to be Christian. He began in southern Norway. "Those who opposed him he punished severely, killing some, mutilating others, and driving some into banishment." He took prisoner Eyvind, a sorcerer, who had dealt with evil spirits. "He put a pan of glowing coals on Eyvind's belly, which burst asunder. Still Eyvind would not accept Christianity, and died." Olaf took all Eyvind's company and "left them bound on a skerry which was under water in flood tide." The people received Christianity, for nobody dared oppose the king's will.

Olaf's zeal extended to Iceland.

Thangbrand was a Saxon priest, a passionate, ungovernable man, and a great manslayer; but he was a good scholar, and a clever man. *The king would not have him in his house upon account of his misdeeds, but he gave him the errand to go to Iceland, and bring that country to the Christian faith.*

Olaf had been a violent viking who knew too well the use of force. Is it always unhealthy to look at the depths to which human nature can descend? In his frenzy for saving souls and exterminating the heathen, the king took the recalcitrant "Raud, bound him to a beam of wood, with a round pin between his teeth to force his mouth open, and put an adder into his mouth, which gnawed its way out of his side, and thus Raud perished." Olaf at moments seems to have been as depraved as any Nazi in a liquidation camp.

The king was thought to suffer from demons, but was it rather from a troubled conscience? Some prefer to think only of how good-looking King Olaf was, and how he exceeded all men in strength and skills, and could throw two spears at once, juggle three swords, and walk on the bulwark of a ship or on the outside of a ship on the oars while his men were rowing. *Heimskringla* says: "Witches and evil spirits tormented King Olaf's men, and sometimes himself, but we will rather write about what occurred when . . . he advanced Christianity."

At Nidaros, the bondes threatened Olaf. *Olaf proposed to meet them at midsummer sacrifice in Maeren [the temple town]. There Olaf said: "If I turn again to sacrifice, I will make the greatest of sacrifices that are in use; and I will sacrifice men. But I will not select slaves or malefactors for this, but will take the greatest men to be offered to the gods, and for this I select. . . ." [He named eleven of the principal men.] The bondes submitted. The king kept all these bondes as hostages until their sons, brothers, and other near relatives came to him. Then Olaf went with bondes into the temple, and lifted up his gold-inlaid ax and struck Thor so that the image rolled down from its seat. Then the king's men turned to and threw down all the gods from their seats.*

When the king came forth from the temple, he offered the bondes two conditions—accept Christianity or fight with him. Then all were baptized, and Olaf took hostages from them for their remaining true to Christianity.

Too violent to be King Olaf's house guest, but held worthy of being a missionary, Thangbrand had proclaimed Christianity in Iceland and many chiefs there had allowed themselves to be baptized. Many more spoke against it. Thangbrand had killed three men during his two years in Iceland. He returned to Norway a few weeks before Leif Erikson reached Nidaros. He told the king how the heathen in Iceland were great sorcerers who had caused the earth to burst asunder under his horse and swallowed it up. When Olaf heard this, "he was so angry he seized all the Icelanders in Nidaros and threw them into dungeons and wanted to have them slain. Then two, Gizur and Hjalti, stepped forward and offered to go surety, and sail to Iceland to preach the faith." As a result, all but the two Icelanders were held pending the outcome.

Thus the pattern was laid for the reception and education of Leif Erikson, heathen captain of a ship who hailed from Greenland and asked to talk with the king. Leif was no doubt fascinated by Olaf's physical prowess. He was perhaps less fascinated when he was made to understand that he would have to become a Christian or go to jail. His father would be furious if Leif accepted baptism. But King Olaf told him that Christ was a greater hero than Thor, because Christ had raided hell and bound the old god of thunder. What could Erik the Red answer to that?

While he was being pressed to make his decision, young Leif could not show any fear of the consequences of refusal, for no man of self-respect could display cowardice. Leif no doubt was given and took time to deliberate. He wisely chose to yield to the king's persuasion, and he and all his men were baptized. For eight days thereafter he wore a white robe and a white cloth band around his head after anointment with the chrism. The rituals and external forms had their effect upon the impressionable youth.

Throughout the winter Leif remained with King Olaf, and as he heard the preachings of the gospel, began to absorb them. The *Heimskringla* says:

> Upon one occasion the king asked Leif whether he intended to return to Greenland the next summer. Leif said yes, if the king was willing. Then said Olaf: "You shall go on a mission for me, to preach Christianity there." Leif said that was a matter for the king's decision, but that he himself foresaw it would be difficult to be a successful missionary in Greenland. The king told Leif there was no man better fitted for the task, and that in his hands the holy cause would surely prosper. "That can only be," Leif said, "if I am supported by the grace of your protection." The king promised protection, and arranged for Leif to take a priest with him.

No doubt the king hinted that only if Greenland were Christianized would he consider sending the trading ships for which Leif had asked.

There can be doubt about whether Leif Erikson's conversion was entirely wholehearted at first, but as an active propagandist for the new faith he became a sincere believer. The very opposition tended to make him so. He had chosen between his father's god Thor and King Olaf's Christ, and his own conviction grew as he worked for the triumph of the side he had been forced to take.

In the spring of the year 1000 Leif Erikson set sail to face his father in Greenland.

10

Leif Goes Exploring

In September, 1000, Leif Erikson landed in Eriksfjörd. We can only guess what he said to his father, or his father to him.

Thor had fiery red hair and beard, and perhaps Erik, with his own red hair, fancied that the physical resemblance strengthened an unbreakable bond between him and his favorite god. In his preference for Thor above all the other gods, Erik was to a large extent monotheistic. In his faith in a god representing the spirit of resistance against inimical forces of nature, he had a certain metaphysical insight. But lusty Thor with his hammer seemed to him stronger than the gentle Christ. He feared the religion of gentleness would weaken his sons. He knew life in Greenland was hard and had to be met with hardness if they were to survive. Besides, if Greenlanders accepted the new faith, his own authority would be threatened. Yet despite his opposition, the new religion spread rapidly. Erik's wife Thorhilda became a Christian and so did her sons. Erik's word for the priest Leif had brought to Greenland was "trickster." A few conservative friends in the fjords stood with Erik.

Erik was at odds with those nearest and dearest to him. His wife tried to convert him, and the saga tells us she used the strongest persuader she knew, denial of sexual relations. Even that deprivation Erik would endure for Thor's sake. What kind of a man did she think he was? Would he deny his beliefs just for her? He was stubborn. Isolated in his own family, he found compensation in a spirit of independence.

His world was going to hell. The Christians were even changing hell. Hell used to be a place where one suffered from icy cold, and now they were saying it was a very hot place where one roasted in fire. As for the Christian Valhalla, their paradise, the priest described it as a land of sunshine and flowers all the year. Erik feared it would make his colonists dissatisfied with Greenland. But Erik's problems were just beginning.

The year after Leif's return to Greenland, Bjarni Herjulfsson sailed on a trading voyage to Norway. This was his first voyage since he had given up voyaging when he joined his father in Greenland. But now his father was dead. The dearth of trading ship arrivals and the increasing shortage of goods convinced Bjarni that trade with Norway would be immensely profitable. In Norway, Bjarni was well received. King Olaf had been killed in battle less than six months after Leif's departure. The earl who thereupon assumed the throne befriended Bjarni, and Bjarni returned to Greenland in 1002 as the "earl's man."

Immediately Bjarni's name was the talk of all the fjords. When he had told the Norwegians about his voyage fifteen years earlier, during which he had not gone ashore on any of the three new lands he saw, "many thought he lacked curiosity and for this reason he was somewhat slandered." There had been similar criticism in Greenland when Bjarni had first returned and told people of his discoveries. But the talk had dropped, for the colonists had been busy clearing fields and building their houses and barns. Until timber became a problem and the inadequate trade was severely felt, the Greenlanders had been content. But now "there was much speaking of land-seeking." Time was ripe for someone to explore the new lands. Leif decided to do it.

Leif made a quick trip 100 miles down the coast to Herjulfsnes. There he questioned Bjarni about the three lands and how to find them. He bought Bjarni's ship. He no doubt took on as part of his crew some of the men who had voyaged with Bjarni fifteen years earlier. Upon returning to Eriksfjörd, he made final preparations. He completed his crew of thirty-five men with some young acquaintances and a Southern man (a German) called Tyrker.

The name Tyrker was the viking equivalent of the German name Dietrich or Dirk. A former retainer of Erik's, Tyrker was the man who had concealed Leif from Erik's enemies in Iceland and acted as the child's foster father during Erik's exile. He and Leif had great affection for each other. At the time of the expedition he must have been at least forty years old.

Leif invited his father to accompany them as leader of the expedition. Their ties were so close that the young man could not find it in his heart to break with Erik. But Erik begged off because, as he said, he felt "no longer able as of yore to endure the troubles of the sea." Leif then appealed to the old man's pride by suggesting that Erik "might with best luck rule them, the kinsmen."

This was a shrewd challenge. Erik was forced to say that he would go, for if he refused, if he spoke his mind about the venture, the Greenlanders would have their minds turned to the warmer southland all the more. Erik had to appear to favor the expedition and to be ready to lead it. But in the end he found an excuse for not going.

At last the day came for Leif's departure from the landing place near the booths and warehouses. Erik, claiming stiffness in the joints, insisted on riding a horse from the house to the ship, a distance of less than a quarter mile. Then, where loose stones on the ground made it seem plausible, he toppled off the horse. To the men who came running, he said the horse slipped and threw him and his foot was hurt. This was clearly an omen! The god Thor did not favor his discovery of other lands. The *Flateyjarbok* quotes Erik as saying: "It is not my fate to find more lands than this where we now dwell. You and I may no longer follow together." In former days this decision would have deterred everyone from the voyage. But Leif and his men were not afraid. They took up the gangplank and raised sail.

Leif had good reason not to attempt to reverse Bjarni's northeastward course through the Strait of Belle Isle. The prevailing winds in the strait in summer were, as Bjarni had reported, from the southwest. In any case, Leif wanted to see what Bjarni had not seen—the eastern side of the great island. Bjarni had indicated that winds and currents on the east side of the island would carry one southward. This hint regarding prevailing winds would be a dominant factor in Leif's choice of route. It is safe to deduce that he aimed for a landfall on the east coast of Newfoundland. That he did make this landfall on the eastern side of the northern peninsula of the island is clear from the *Flateyjarbok*. It is to this saga we turn for the account of Leif's famous voyage.

They found first that land which Bjarni found last. There they sailed to land and cast anchor and put out the boat and went ashore and saw there no grass. Large ice mountains were seen far away, and from the sea to the ice mountains all was flat rock, and this land seemed to them to be good for nothing. Then said Leif: "Unlike Bjarni, we have stepped ashore on this land, and I will now give it a name, and call it Helluland [Flat Rock Land]."

The revealing details are that they entered a harbor ("cast anchor and put out the boat"), that they "saw there no grass," that "large ice mountains were seen far away," and that from the sea to the distant mountains the land appeared flat and infertile.

From talks with Newfoundlanders familiar with the coasts and from study of the large-scale maps, one and one-quarter inches to a mile, produced by the Department of Mines and Technical Surveys of Canada, National Topographic Series, I found Leif's probable landing place. The Long Range Mountains run close to the western side of the northern peninsula, and cattle graze on the meadows near the coast. Dr. V. S. Papezik, assistant professor of Geology at Memorial University of Newfoundland, explained that these mountains are part of the Appalachian chain, rounded with much erosion

that has left fertile soil near their bases. On the east coast of
the peninsula the geology is very different, for we find there
raised beaches of gravel from which the soil has been washed
away.

There are three harbors along less than thirty miles of the
east coast where Leif may have cast anchor. The most northerly of these is Canada Bay, sixty-five miles south of the northern tip of Newfoundland. The other two are Hooping
Harbour and Fourché Harbour (Williamsport). Fourché Harbour is almost entirely surrounded by woods, and so does not
fit the saga description. Hooping Harbour fits the description
somewhat better. However, on the high ground above the
harbor there are only small patches of barren ground, inter-
spersed with areas of forest. The hinterland is hardly "flat,"
since the land rises 500 feet in the first ten miles from the
heights above shore. A fourth, but most unlikely possibility, is
Orange Bay (Harbour Deep). However, if Leif had coasted
that far south, he would have changed course to the eastward
after sighting Partridge Point to the southeast.

This leaves Canada Bay as the most probable site of Leif's
landing. Leif could not have failed to see its entrance, which
is two miles wide. Four miles inside the bay to the northwest
is Otter Cove. This would have invited a landing, for it is
perfectly sheltered from the ocean and offers a gradual slope
from its shore up to a broad infertile area at 1,000-foot altitude
and to the west. That infertile area is at least five miles wide,
and to the west of it the land looks flat, for there is an average
rise of only 100 feet in the first ten miles. Beyond in the distance, mountains with snow fields near their summits rise to
altitudes of 1,989, 1,710, 1,480, and 2,128 feet. These peaks are
visible "far away" to the west and southwest at a distance
from the Canada Bay beholder of 30, 21, 28, and 47 miles,
respectively.

At the time Leif Erikson landed at or near Canada Bay,
there was a viking settlement near L'Anse-aux-Meadow, at the
northern tip of Newfoundland. The husband of the archaeologist who unearthed that settlement thinks northern Newfoundland was Leif Erikson's third land. My reasons for not

thinking so, together with a theory about how vikings had settled near L'Anse-aux-Meadow, will be found in Appendix II.

After Leif had named the island, he followed the eastern and southern shores probably to within sight of the southwestern corner of Newfoundland, which Bjarni's men would have recognized. Having come to where the coast turns north, Leif had supplemented and confirmed Bjarni's discovery by completing the viking circumnavigation of the great island. The following year Leif returned home to Greenland by Bjarni's west coast route.

The saga continues with Leif's voyage after he named Flat Rock Land.

Leif and his men went to the ship, put to sea and found a second land, and here also they sailed in close and cast anchor, and put out the boat and got ashore. This was a level land, completely wooded, with broad stretches of white sand; and the shore region where they went did not slant steeply toward the sea. Leif then said: "This land shall have a name in accordance with its nature and shall be called Markland [Forestland]." After that they went back to the ship as fast as possible.

Their haste was to take advantage of a favorable northeast wind that had begun to blow.

Leif's words "level land, completely wooded" perfectly describe Nova Scotia when seen from the ocean south of it. Several of the Nova Scotia beaches are from a quarter- to a half-mile wide. It may be imagined that such beaches were tremendously impressive to men who had seen nothing comparable in Greenland. In the accounts of Leif's brief visit the words "where they went" indicate that he and his men actually saw only a very limited area. The shore which "did not slant steeply toward the sea" contrasted with the generally steep shores of Greenland and Newfoundland.

The stand of timber in Nova Scotia was also impressive

in those days. Though the primeval forest exists no longer, even in inland patches, some idea of it may be gathered from the British Admiralty's eighteenth-century ruling that all trees there over a hundred feet in height were the property of the Royal Navy, to be used for masts.

Whether or not the lettering on a stone at Yarmouth, Nova Scotia, is a runic inscription left by Leif Erikson and his men on the occasion of his naming the land, or when he stopped in Nova Scotia on his return trip, or by someone else at some other time, Leif's stated reason for naming Markland carried a slur at his father Erik for having coined the name Greenland. Olaf Strandwold translates the Yarmouth inscription as "Leif to Erik raises [this monument]." [1] We may be sure that Leif's men did not fail to see the humor in their leader, as well as his honesty, and there was no doubt much appreciative laughter and applause.

---

[1] *Norse Runic Inscriptions Along the Atlantic Seaboard*, pp. 80–88. See the discussion of this inscription and translation in my book *Atlantic Crossings Before Columbus*, pp. 204–7.

11

The Third Land

Geographical discoveries happen by accident. It was so with the viking discoveries of the Faeroes, Iceland, Greenland, and Bjarni's discoveries of Newfoundland and the lands southwest of Newfoundland. On the other hand, explorations happen by intent—by the intent of inquiring minds.

Leif Erikson had such a mind. And perhaps more important he had the ability to lead. About twenty-five years of age in the year 1003, he did all the things his men did, and he could do them better. His judgment was so superior that his men called the consequences "happy" and "lucky." The saga describes him as "a very tall man and a very moderate man in all regards."

Leif and his men sailed from Markland with a north-easter, using Bjarni's sailing directions in reverse. They were "out" for two days before they saw land. There has been continued and widespread disagreement about where Leif Erikson landed and made his camp that winter. (The theories are listed in Appendix I.) This is the more strange since the *Flateyjarbok* gives detailed descriptions of the landing site. Moreover, several viking expeditions subsequently reached Leif's campsite, using information supplied by Bjarni and Leif. The narratives of the later explorers help pinpoint the exact location.

Here is the *Flateyjarbok* account of Leif Erikson's arrival at the third land:

Now they sailed from thence [the second land] on the open ocean before a northeaster and were out for two days before they saw land. They sailed to this land and came to an island which lay to the north of the land. They went ashore on this island and looked about them. It proved a fair day, and they found dew on the grass, and when they wet their fingers with the dew and put their fingers to their mouths, they felt they had never tasted anything so sweet. Afterward they went to their ship and sailed into a sound that lay between the island and that cape which extended to the north from the land, steering to the west of the cape. It was very shallow there at ebb tide, and their ship stood there grounded, and it was a long distance to look from the ship to the sea. Yet they were so curious to go ashore that they could not wait for the tide to rise under their ship, but they ran the boat to the land, into a river that flowed down from a lake. But as soon as the tide rose under their ship, they took the boat and rowed to the ship and conveyed it up the river, and into the lake and there cast anchor. They carried their leather bags [sleeping bags] ashore and built temporary shelters [literally, "booths"].

They built their shelters on Cape Cod. The first view Leif had was of its east or "back" side with nearby Monomoy, that runs for nine and one-half miles to the south. Cape Cod with its breaker-swept sand bars off shore hardly presented a safe coast to approach in a northeast storm. Leif was in a desperate situation. Coming toward the land obliquely from the northeast, he had no choice but to stay in the offing if he could, and to coast southward. Because of the wind direction, he could not turn northward. He and his men may have sighted the cape at night, but more probably just before dusk. They looked for a break in the shore where they could find shelter in the lea of land. Beyond the south end of Monomoy they found a broad opening through which they entered. The northeast wind did not permit them to turn northward into the lea of Monomoy. They could turn only to the south,

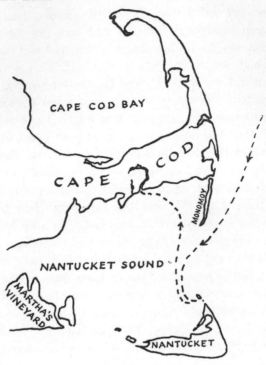

Leif Erikson was twenty-four when he set out to explore
new lands. Unable to persuade his father, Erik the Red,
to go along, he left him in Greenland and sailed south
with a crew of thirty-five men. He put ashore briefly at
Newfoundland, Nova Scotia, and Nantucket. Then,
reaching Cape Cod, he sailed up the Bass River and
built a temporary shelter at Follins Pond.

where by good fortune they came into the lee of a small island
which is known as Great Point of Nantucket. There they anchored for the night.

As soon as dawn came they went ashore. They found that
the island consisted of sand dunes with sparse scrub vegetation. In the midst of the dunes was a grass area, a level depres-
sion covered with tall grass. The northeaster had blown itself
out; in the sun glistened a white wetness on (Norse a—which

may mean also "in" or "among") the grass. This wetness was not precisely "dew," as Leif and his men with their limited knowledge called it; it was raindrops on the grass blades and rain water in a small pool actually below the level of high tide. A marvel to Leif and his men, they may have considered it a good omen. The rain water tasted sweet by contrast with the stale water in their ship casks after two weeks or more on their voyage from Greenland.

The vikings climbed the highest dune to look around. The island they were on was about three-quarters of a mile long and at most 200 yards wide. The local level of the ocean that had been raised by the northeaster and by the high tide that early morning, as will be demonstrated, deeply covered the narrow sand bar for the first two miles to the south of them. The ocean was flowing into the inland water. Beyond the two miles of water ran a narrow ridge of dunes for another three miles, and five miles due south of the island on which they stood was land that extended as far as they could see to the southwest. They naturally assumed that land—Nantucket—to be part of the mainland, and could not know that it was itself an island. When they got home a year later, they told their listeners in Greenland that they had landed on an island that lay to the north of "the land." For a description of the sand bar and dunes, and facts which amply justify acceptance of approximately the same local conditions one thousand years ago as now, see my book *The Lost Discovery*, pages 53–54.

As it was important to see as far as possible what lay ahead in inland waters, Leif's men made a human tower raising the lookout man's eyes ten or twelve feet above the dune. The lookout man was probably Leif, who had the best eyesight. From where he stood he could see the south end of Monomoy, but nothing of Cape Cod to the north. However, since with a "fair day" after a northeaster the wind was now blowing from the southeast and shifting south, Leif and his men sailed from Great Point across Nantucket Sound toward the north. They knew land was in that direction, because they had seen land north of Monomoy before they came in from the ocean.

Soon, as they sailed northward, they began to see treetops and the highest hills of the Barnstable Peninsula. They sailed close to the south shore of Cape Cod and coasted westward, looking for an opening in the land. They sailed thus for four or five hours from the Great Point of Nantucket, until they came to the Bass River, a sizable stream.

Approaching the mouth of the Bass River, the ship, which drew about three and a half to four feet, went aground on a sandy shallow. The ship was in no danger, as Leif's men instantly determined from the nature of the bottom, but the tide was ebbing and would continue ebbing for another two hours. This meant that the ship would be stuck for about four hours until the incoming tide floated her again. Leif and his men could not wait. They were eager to learn where the river led. Some of them took the afterboat and sailed her into and up the river against the tide. By now the wind had for some hours been blowing steadily from the southwest. In about an hour they came to a lake five and a half miles inland. Now called Follins Pond, this lake was three quarters of a mile long and a half mile wide. To the left, along the southern shore, Leif's men found a promising site for a camp—shelter from the wind, with fresh water at the shore from a most copious spring.

Having estimated very closely at what hour the incoming tide would float the ship free, they knew when to start the return down river. But against the now-incoming tide and the prevailing wind, they could not use the afterboat sail. They had to "row back to the ship."

Those who had remained on the ship had meanwhile made two observations. One was that at low tide it was "very shallow there" around the ship. That is, a shallow depth of water remained around the ship. The ship was not left high and dry on an exposed mud flat, as some interpreters of the saga have carelessly asserted.

The other observation was most important because it gave future mariners the final sailing direction to Leif's campsite. From the mast of the ship when aground, the lookout had seen to the east the dunes of narrow Monomoy gleaming in the sunlight of the early afternoon, and Leif and his men knew that the ocean lay just beyond those dunes. The lookout reported that from the mast height "it was a long distance to look to the sea." The word *sia* (salt water), used so soon after *sund* (sound), did not refer to the river water close to the ship, but to the now-distant ocean. The mast-height horizon visibility, as we know, was seven and a half miles. The twenty- to thirty-foot dunes on Monomoy could be seen above the horizon for six miles. The lookout on the stationary ship would have seen them if they were seven and a half plus six miles away. The actual distance from the mouth of the Bass River to Monomoy is twelve miles, close to the limit of visibility for the lookout. It was, indeed, "a long distance to look." Back in Greenland a year later, Leif and his men used practical terms to tell mariners how far they would have to sail westward from the ocean into Nantucket Sound in order to reach the mouth of the river that would take them up to Leif's camp.

With the incoming tide and the prevailing southwest wind, Leif and his men sailed the ship up the Bass River to Follins Pond in little more than one hour. There they dropped anchor in the lee of the fifty-foot heights along the south shore of the lake. They went ashore with their "leather bags." About twelve hours had elapsed since dawn. They had an hour or two of daylight in which to build temporary shelters.

They spent their first week or two busily fishing "in the river and in the lake" for the plentiful salmon "larger than they had ever seen," which they smoked in great quantities for winter food. According to the U.S. Fish and Wildlife Service, when there were salmon at the latitude of Cape Cod, the salmon ceased running about the end of the first week in September. Leif's arrival in North America was not, as was once supposed, late in September, but late in August. Now that the United States of America has a Leif Erikson Day, it should be noted that its date, October 9, is the date when the first Norwegian immigrant ship entered New York Harbor in 1825. However, coming just before Columbus Day, it does remind us of Leif's prior discovery of America.

Leif and his men probably caught salmon at night by a method often used in Norway. A fire is lit a few feet above the water. Attracted by the light, the salmon jam against each other close to the light. In shallows, the backs of many salmon are out of the water. Men standing in the water have only to grab the fish by hand or spear them up.

While their main food needs were being met, Leif and his men carefully considered whether the south shore of Follins Pond was a good place to spend the winter. They were in no haste, for they had more than a month of sailing weather ahead of them to explore farther had they been so minded. But the advantages of the site they had found grew upon them as they investigated. The saga is remarkably specific in essentials, for it says:

> Later on, when they decided to remain there that winter, they built a large house. There seemed to be excellent country thereabouts in which there would be no lack of cattle fodder for the winter. There came no frost in winter, and there was but slight withering of the grass.

The words "a large house" tell us that Leif's house in North America was a one-room hall in which all thirty-five men slept for maximum defense against possible enemies. They took no chances by splitting up their numbers in several small houses. This fact has not been understood by some who have misinterpreted the name by which Leif's camp was called, "Leif's Shelters." It was called "Shelters," plural, because, in addition to the hall, there was of course the other necessary shelter—the shed housing their ship until the spring.[1]

---

[1] Several times in reference to Leif Erikson's campsite the saga mentions "buildings" and "houses," plural, but Cleasby, Vigfusson, and Craigie in *An Icelandic-English Dictionary*, under the word *hús* [house] point out that "in olden times" there was "the frequent use of the plural even when referring to a single house."

Leif and his men had to bring the ship ashore and lodge
it for the winter under cover. They had to keep rain and snow
out of it during freezing weather, so that ice would not form
inside and split the planking. It was even more imperative
that they protect it from drying winds. Major William Smyth
of Noank, Connecticut, who has had more experience than
anyone I know in the shoring of ships, tells me that drying
out would do more serious damage than ice. Drying out, or

After a decision to winter at Follins Pond, Leif's men built
a large hall for themselves and a shed to protect their ship.
Some years later, two Icelandic brothers named Helgi and
Finnbogi came to the new land with Leif's sister Freydis.
They built shelters nearby at Mill Pond.

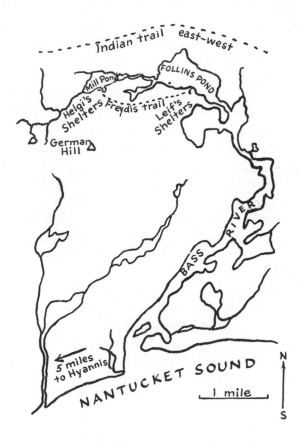

dry rot, would cause rapid deterioration of the wood and would open many seams. For this reason, Leif and his men would haul the ship out as late as possible in the fall, and put her overboard again as early as possible in the spring. The sagas always mention that it was in the spring that the vikings made a ship ready, presumably long before they sailed.

All the time that the ship was out of the water they had to keep it on even keel. They could not careen it; for the edge of the gunwale was not strong enough to support the ship's weight.

Stripped of gear, except for the unstepped mast which was probably not removed, the ship weighed as much as thirteen or fourteen tons, far too heavy for Leif's thirty-five men to lift. But they did not rely entirely upon brawn in hauling out the ship.

They selected a shelving beach leading up to a place just above the highest tides, where they leveled the ground. There they laid flat stones at intervals in a row, to serve as the bases for keel bearings.

How did they get the ship up and onto these bearings? After lightening the ship of its gear, they brought the forward end of the keel to the edge of the shelving beach. Then many of the crew crowded far aft in the ship, their weight trimming the ship so that the forward end of the keel was raised and could be nosed up on the beach above rollers placed to receive it. In a viking ship, as in the case of a primitive skin boat with keel attached, the keel made possible the hauling ashore and the relaunching. The keel, which gave the ship its longitudinal strength, took all the strains and tensions during the hauling out.

The crew faced the mechanical problem of dragging the ship on rollers up the incline to the prepared level. They applied force with a sideways heaving by as many as ten men to each side, with their backs against the planking and their rumps under the bilge. This was the only position possible for these men since the gunwale, about seven feet above the keel, was too high to be gripped effectively. The men at the sides in their heaving and surging forward could not lift the ship's weight, but propelled the ship forward on the rollers by making their moves in unison, stepping sideways in time with a chant which gave rhythm. Their utmost efforts were not more than barely sufficient to move the ship a few inches up the incline with each rhythmic heave. Their back-straining task was very likely eased by the power of a windlass.

They had two possible ways of attaching the windlass hawser to the ship. One was by a bight of the rope around a short iron pin inserted into a horizontal hole through the front end of the keel. The other was by a sling around the entire length of the ship, to pull the sternpost, but this would require more length of rope than the ship probably carried.

The windlass was an effective power plant, operated by four men with bars. It could apply tension to the breaking point of any hawser the vikings had. Leif probably had a good hawser of white flax, which was somewhat similar to hemp. The incline up into the shoring site at Leif's Shelters was a 1-in-14 grade. This estimate is based on the fact that the floating ship drew about 3½ feet, and when shored its keel was about 2 feet above the highest tides. The ship had therefore been raised 5½ feet in a distance of 75 feet. When the ship reached the height of the intended shoring place, the windlass was no longer needed, for the muscle power of the men could readily overcome the friction inertia of the rollers on the level.

When the ship was in position above the flat stones, wedges were driven in by mallet blows from both sides on top of the stones, to raise the keel enough to release the rollers. The hard wood wedges, as well as the rollers, were no doubt standard ship's equipment.

The ship's empty water casks topped with short planks, and stakes inclined inward to abut against the bottom edges of overlapping strakes, served to hold the shored vessel on even keel. With plenty of slender trees from which to make roof beams, Leif and his men erected a shed for the ship, undoubtedly with peaked roof to withstand the weight of whatever snows might come.

After several weeks, when the keel bearings had "settled," the flat stones were practically flush with the ground. These would be left undisturbed with their tops in perfect level for use in subsequent winters. In drawing the ship out of the shed for relaunching, care would be taken so that the rollers would not disarrange the keel bearings. If necessary, the keel-bearing stones would be temporarily removed, and after the ship had been withdrawn would be replaced in the settled depressions.

Convincing proof that Leif and his men were more than capable in their knowledge and skill in hauling out and re-launching the ship is found in the saga, in Leif's counseling his brother Thorvald the next year to take only thirty men.

In building his "large house" Leif seems to have had in mind the pattern of his father's hall. In accordance with viking custom, he erected his house on a height where it commanded a view of the lake and of the river approach to the lake. Leif and his men thought in terms of waterways by which attackers might come. They did not know whether the people who inhabited the wilderness would attack them, and they were fortunate in that their presence remained undetected by the natives. No Indians were seen at Leif's camp for a period of four years. The map of the region shows how this could be.

In the first place, Leif's camp on the south shore of Follins Pond was on what was almost an island. The only dry-ground approach was through a narrow gap between marshes to the southwest of German Hill. The whole area, bounded by the Bass River, Follins Pond, Mill Pond, and the waterways to the west of German Hill, was practically cut off from the rest of Cape Cod. This was an area into which natives on foot were unlikely to enter, for to leave it they would have to retrace their steps. Moreover, Indians disliked getting into marshes, and the ponds and marshes were more extensive a thousand years ago when the ocean level was about twenty-five to thirty inches higher than it is now. The Bass River waterway was the remains of a channel that had at one time crossed the cape. In earliest post-Columbian times, the Bass

River region was a sort of no man's land between the Matta-kiest tribe to the west and the Nobsquassets and Monomoy-icks to the east. Waterways were tribal boundaries on the cape in three other places also. From the locations elsewhere of Indian burials and shell heaps, the indications are that the Bass River area had always been a tribal boundary.

To avoid crossing the Bass River waterway, the Indians used an east-west trail out of sight of the ponds at some distance north of them. At its nearest, the trail was two thirds of a mile from Leif's camp. Indians who used it did not turn aside to Follins Pond because they had good salt-water fishing elsewhere. A north-south trail from Hyannis to Yarmouth ran to the west of the marshes at the west end of Mill Pond. It was miles from Leif's camp.

Leif and his men had chosen their winter campsite perceptively. They most certainly found the east-west Indian trail, and they may have explored along it far enough to discover that there were savages on the cape living a few miles to the west, and that there was only the trail between. They probably saw the smoke of Indian campfires. Conscious of their small numbers, they may have refrained until after dark on clear days from making a fire that would send up a column of smoke.

Leif and his men explored the nearest hills. From the surface of Follins Pond, toward its north side, they could see the top of German Hill, an elevation of 135 feet. From Mill Pond they were within a mile of the summit. After an easy climb they had a view of Nantucket Sound, the tops of the trees on Nantucket Island, and part of Martha's Vineyard.

From Black Ball Hill, 159 feet in elevation, less than a mile and a half north of Follins Pond, Leif and his men saw Cape Cod Bay and the Massachusetts coast. When they saw the inward-curving point directly to the north of them, where the city of Provincetown now is, they learned that their camp was on a cape extending eastward and then northward.

From what they saw in two short half-day excursions on foot to the nearby hills and on the day of their arrival, Leif and his men learned the general outline of Cape Cod. They had surveying views over land and water about fifty miles north-south, and about thirty-five miles east-west. Leif inevitably realized that he could explore the region farther only by making very long expeditions away from camp. Apparently he chose to keep his men close to camp for mutual protection. Though this may seem overcautious, his ruling made good sense.

After the house was built, Leif divided his followers into two groups: one to remain at camp, the other to explore the country. The members of the exploring party were to keep in sight of each other and to return home each evening. Leif alternately went with the exploring group and remained behind.

It was after this routine had been established that Leif's foster father, Tyrker, was reported missing one evening. Leif immediately led a dozen men in a search for the old man. However, the missing man met them with high excitement a short distance from the hall. The scene affected Leif so deeply that he related it in great detail a year afterward when telling of his exploration. So the incident has been preserved for all time.

Leif at once observed that his foster father was excited. He [Tyrker] had a large forehead, restless eyes, and small freckles, and though he was a puny, insignificant-looking fellow, he was a leader in martial sports.

Leif asked him: "Why art thou so late, my foster father, and separated from thy comrades?"

For the first few moments Tyrker spoke in the southern tongue, rolling his eyes, and making wry faces, and they could not understand him. After a little he explained to them in Norse: "I did not walk far beyond the others, but I have news for you. I have found grapevines and grapes!"

"Are you certain, foster father?" asked Leif.

"Most certain," said he, "for I was born where there is no lack of grapevines and grapes."

After a night's sleep, Leif in the morning said to his shipmates: "From now on we have two things to do, and every
day we shall either gather grapes, or cut vinewood [vin-vid—
stems of vines] and chop down trees to make a lading for my
ship."

This they did, and it is said their afterboat was filled with
grapes.

Wild grapes on Cape Cod began to ripen in the second
half of August. Grapes were something entirely new to Greenlanders, and with great enthusiasm Leif's men picked as many
grapes as they could, using their afterboat as a temporary
receptacle. That early fall they no doubt made some wine. By
Christmas, Leif and his men had probably finished drinking
most or all of the wine they had made, though Leif may have
kept a sample to carry home. Neither grapes nor wine were
later mentioned as part of his cargo, which consisted of timber
felled in the fall and vinestems to be used as withies. The
northern limit of wild vines, be it noted, was at 47° North,
which is south of Newfoundland. Although the saga uses the
same word vin-vid for both grapevines and withies, grapevines are too fragile to make satisfactory withies. Greenbrier
vines, which grow in profusion on Cape Cod, however, would
have made excellent ones.

Because of its many thorns, from a half inch to an inch
long, greenbrier is popularly called "stay awhile." It is as
persuasive as barbed wire. Rabbits can escape pursuers into a
clump of greenbrier, since its thorns will rip the hide of any
sizable dog attempting to follow. An old story has it that a
pioneer fleeing from Indians got caught in greenbrier and
preferred to stop and be killed rather than try to tear his way
through. Near Follins Pond I have seen hundreds of strands of
the fierce brier hanging close together over the branches of a
single tree, like lianas in a tropical forest, almost completely
veiling the tree.

The thorns of greenbrier may be readily stripped off with
a knife, and three stripped briers, which may be fifteen to

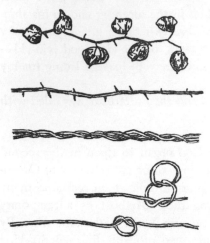

Greenbrier vines, called "Stay Awhile" because of their long, sharp thorns, can be made into tremendously strong and flexible ropes. The drawing shows them with their leaves, with their thorns, and stripped, knotted, and braided. These vines made up half of Leif's cargo—the other half was timber.

twenty feet long, when braided together, make a flexible rope of tremendous strength. A braid of three briers, each averaging a fifth of an inch in diameter, will support the weight of several men. I had such a braided length tested at the engineering laboratory of Columbia University. It withstood a pull of 510 pounds before the fibers began to stretch. Braids of any greater number of strands can be made to produce a hawser of any required strength. Additional lengths can be braided in, with the junctions strengthened by interlacings and even by knots of thinner fresh stems of the brier, so that a rope may be made of any desired length. The proved strength of greenbrier is one third that of the best Manila rope of the same diameter. When I showed Dr. Johannes Brøndsted greenbrier braids, he said he at last understood Leif's order to "cut vines."

Leif had already named one land for its forests, and the forests on Cape Cod were not unique. Trees on Cape Cod, most of them ten to twelve inches in diameter, and the largest in Leif's day about two feet, were of a size the Greenlanders wanted. It was not the trees, however, that caused Leif to name the country. The saga says: "Leif gave the land a name born from its products [plural]; he called it Vinland."

Leif had in mind two products: vinestems and grapes. The name Vinland had double significance; it meant Land of Vines and Wineland. In the naming, Leif was completely honest, yet one meaning gave some vikings an illusion that was never realized. To vikings, a wineland was a feaster's dream. The lack of wine in Greenland, except for what was imported, was a reason for Leif's stress on wineberries.

In Leif's Vinland tall bright green salt-meadow grass (*Distichlis spicata*) grew in the marshy areas, many of which are now cranberry bogs. With roots in mud soaked by tidal water, the salt grass or fresh grass "slightly withered" during the winter. This appears to contradict Leif's statement that "there came no frost in winter." It must be remembered, however, that Leif and his men were accustomed to the fierce winters of Greenland. They would scarcely notice a snowfall of a few inches or a slight frost. As a matter of fact, the average winter on Cape Cod is much milder than in other parts of Massachusetts. On the cape light falls of snow usually melt in the mild ocean atmosphere within a few hours.

During the winter in Vinland, Leif and his men made an astronomical observation. The saga says: "The days and nights were more nearly of equal length than in Greenland or Iceland. On the shortest day in winter the sun had *Eyktarstad* [touched the horizon in setting at S. 60° W.] and *Dagmalastad* [rose at E. 30° S.]."

Gustav Storm and H. Geelmuyden show that *Eyktarstad* is an azimuth of the sun. The vikings divided the quarter circle from South to West into three parts, and *Eyktarstad* was two thirds of that distance, or 60° West of South. As Alan L. Binns [2] points out:

It is clear from the use of "eyktarstadr" (S. 60° W.) in the description of Vinland's position that the vikings had not only an understanding of the connection between the sun's amplitude and altitude and a given latitude, but also some means of establishing the azimuth corresponding to "eyktarstadr" with-

[2] In his Introduction to Holger Arbman, *The Vikings*.

out reference to familiar landmarks. . . . Some sort of bearing dial would be required for this. . . . Some such device was used.

The syllable "Eykt" includes both the hour and the meal farmers ate at that hour, 4:30 P.M., afternoon meal. The sun sets at Follins Pond on the shortest day in winter at 4:31 P.M. The latitude of Leif's campsite at Follins Pond is 41° 42′ 20″.

The saga says: *When the spring came they made their ship ready, and sailed away.*

In the spring, as was customary, Leif and his men made necessary repairs on their ship, calked, and relaunched her. The narrative is laconic, and the additional words "and sailed away" do not compel us to believe that they sailed in the spring. Indeed, the *Flateyjarbok* goes on to say that they sailed "thereafter." Undoubtedly they sailed in the summer, in order to arrive home when the Greenland coast was free of ice.

Thereafter they went to sea and had a fair wind until they saw Greenland and fells [moors] under the glaciers. Then one of the men spoke to Leif: "Why steerest thou the ship so much into the wind?"

Leif replied: "I am taking care of my rudder, but of more than that besides; or what do you see that is remarkable?"

They answered that they saw nothing remarkable.

"I do not know," said Leif, "whether I see a ship or a skerry."

Now they saw it, and said it was a skerry; but he saw sharper than they, for he saw men on the skerry. "Now I will that we beat against the wind," said Leif, "so as to get near to them, to see if they want to be found by us, and whether there is need of giving them assistance. If they are not peacefully inclined, then we shall have the advantage over them."

Now they sailed to the skerry, lowered the sail, and dropped anchor, and put out another little boat [the two-man skiff] which they had with them. Then Tyrker asked: "Who is the leader of your party?"

The leader said: "I am called Thorer, and am a Norseman; but what is thy name?"

Leif told it him.

"Art thou the son of Erik the Red of Brattahlid?" Thorer asked.

Leif replied that he was. "Now," said Leif, "I make you this offer: I will take you all on my ship, and all the goods that the ship will hold."

They accepted those terms, and then they sailed to Eriksfjörd with the lading, until they came to Brattahlid. They unloaded the ship, and then Leif invited Thorer to dwell with him, and Gudrid, his wife, and three other men, but provided dwellings for the other men, both Thorer's and his own. Leif had rescued fifteen men from the skerry. He was thereafter called Leif the Lucky. Leif now had great wealth and was highly honored.

That winter came much sickness among Thorer's men, and Thorer and a great part of his crew died. That winter died also Erik the Red.

Several facts are revealed in the story of Leif's rescue of the shipwrecked Norsemen. One is that Leif had better eyesight than his men. The skerry must have been very close to Eriksfjörd, and the sea could not have been rough, otherwise it would have been disastrous to have taken an additional fifteen people and their property aboard a ship already loaded to capacity. But Leif got home safely with the lading, and "was thereafter called Leif the Lucky." The rescued property was probably his by custom of salvage, and with ready sale of a shipload of timber and withy vines, he "had great wealth."

12

Thorvald Erikson's Explorations

Upon Erik's death Leif became the leading man in Greenland and had to assume responsibilities at Brattahlid thereafter. Further exploring in Vinland remained for Leif's brother Thorvald. He had criticized Leif for having limited his explorations to a half-day's walking distance from his camp. He intended to learn more about what was obviously a very large country.

Now there was much talk of the Vinland voyage of Leif. Thorvald, his brother, held the opinion that the country had not been sufficiently explored. Then Leif said to Thorvald: "Thou shalt go out with my ship, brother, if thou wilt go to Vinland; however, I want the ship to go first for the wood which Thorer had on the skerry." And so it was done. Under Leif's advice, Thorvald prepared for the voyage with a crew of 30 men. They provisioned the ship and put to sea, and there is nothing to be said of their voyage until they arrived in Vinland at Leif's Shelters. They shored their ship there and kept quiet that winter and caught fish for food.

Thorvald and his men knew that the mouth of their river opened into a sound which in large areas was very shallow. From German Hill they could see that sound extending into the land to the west. Thorvald decided not to use the ship for exploring westward, but the afterboat, which drew less water and could be lifted across shallows. The freeboard, though low, would suffice against such waves as they would encounter. A small crew of about ten or a dozen men in a single afterboat had reason to fear possible attacks by the people who inhabited the land, whoever they might be. At night the exploring party naturally would anchor or moor in the lee of an offshore island. The eighteen or twenty men who remained at camp would be busy getting in food for the winter.

In the spring Thorvald ordered that the ship be made ready, and he sent the afterboat and some men with it to go to the western part of the land and explore there during the summer. These men found it a pleasing, well-wooded country, with the woods near the salt water and the white sands. There were many islands and shoals. They found no dwellings of men or lairs of beasts, but in one of the islands to the west they found a corncrib of wood. They found no other works of man. They returned to Leif's Shelters at harvesttime.

Thorvald's men explored along the north side of the inland waters: from Nantucket Sound into Vineyard Sound, Buzzards Bay, Narragansett Bay, and inlets close along the shore of Connecticut. At least it is reasonable to assume that this was their route, since it is the one that a later party avoided. Each subsequent expedition naturally wished not to duplicate earlier findings. The mention of "many islands and shoals" points to the shores of Rhode Island and Connecticut, not to the north shore of Long Island.

In 1007, Thorvald explored the coast on the other side of Leif's camp. Because this meant sailing out into the ocean, Thorvald used the ship and conducted the expedition in person.

The next summer Thorvald went eastward with the trading ship and to the north of the land. Then off a cape they had a hard storm, and being driven on shore there, broke the keel under their ship. There they had a long delay while they repaired their ship. Then Thorvald said to his followers: "I desire that we here erect the old keel on this cape and call it Kjalnar Nes [Keel Cape]," and this they did.

The keel must have been broken on a sandy shore, for rocks would have stove the hull. The ship seems to have been hogged when her middle was momentarily astride a sand bar.

Thorvald and his men had a big job. They had to build a temporary shelter for sleeping and for storing their food. They had to remove everything from the ship and raise it so that they could work under its bottom. They had to cut down a suitable tree, and trim the timber for a new keel. They had to carry the hewn timber to the ship, chip away the broken keel, and fit in the new. Then they had to collect resin from evergreen trees and recalk most of the ship's seams. Men familiar with ship repairing estimate this labor took them at least a month. It suited Thorvald's fancy to leave the old keel as a monument and place marker. It gave him an opportunity to imitate his father and brother in assigning a geographical name.

The temporary damage to the ship involved no change in Thorvald's plan of exploring the coast "to the north." With the ship again seaworthy, as is implied in the words "sailed away from there," he continued sailing to the northward from Keel Cape.

After this they sailed away from there, and to the eastward farther out from land [austr firir landit], and into the mouths of a fjord that was near there, and to a headland which extended out there and was covered with trees.

The saga implies that as long as the coast permitted, Thorvald sailed northward close to shore to observe the nature of the country. This he could do along the coasts of Massachusetts, New Hampshire, and southern Maine. But when he found a coast that held him off with long promontories beetling with cliffs and with many rocky islets far out, he could not longer safely stay close to the land. He then sailed well out in the offing to avoid further damage to the ship. This was the only safe way to sail off the Maine coast to the east of Casco Bay.

Because he was "farther out," he was the more eager to sight high ground from which he might be able to look for a great distance across the land, since the shore did not permit close observation. The low hills on the west side of the

After Leif had returned to Greenland, his brother Thorvald went to Vinland and spent the winter at Follins Pond. Sailing northward the next summer, he entered a fjord, now called Somes Sound, on Mt. Desert Island off the Maine coast.

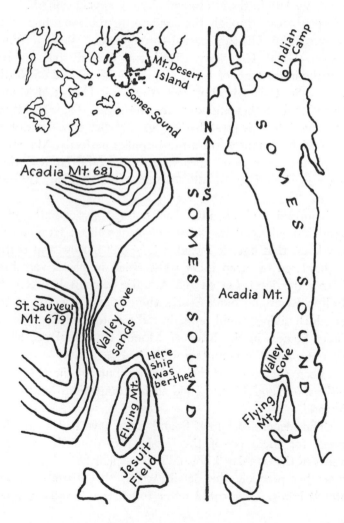

Penobscot are well inland, too far away to have been seen by a lookout at mast height. But the mountains of the Mount Desert range can be seen for more than fifty miles by an observer thirty feet above the sea. As soon as Thorvald's lookout caught sight of that range, Thorvald set his course for it. At a speed of about five knots, it would have taken the ship ten hours from the time they first sighted the range to come close to it. Along that dangerous, rocky coast Thorvald was of course sailing only during daylight hours. The chances are that it was late in the afternoon when Thorvald came in from the open ocean through the sea lane to the mountains that beckoned him. His ship passed through the "Western Way" between Great Cranberry Island and Seawall and entered what the inhabitants of Little Cranberry Island and of Northeast and Southwest Harbors call "the Great Harbor of Mount Desert." There they anchored for the night. There are three entrances into this great harbor, so that the saga description of the *kiafta* (mouths) of a fjord applies perfectly. Moreover, the phrase "near there" suggests that the fjord lay near their course in the offing. In other words, the mountains lay near the sea.

Thorvald and his men had entered the mouths of a "fjord." If vikings knew what any geographical term meant, they knew that one. It meant a long and narrow arm of the sea bordered by steep rocky walls rising in places very high above water level. On all the Atlantic seacoast between the Hudson River and Nova Scotia, there is only one arm of the sea which vikings could properly call a fjord, and that fjord is Somes Sound, in the heart of Mount Desert Island, where salt water laps the mountain walls. The saga says:

There they berthed their ship, and put out the gangplank to the shore, and Thorvald and all his companions went up on the land.

The scenery of Somes Sound must have had a nostalgic appeal for the men of the fjords. Moreover, the dramatic events of the one day Thorvald's men spent there made them remember precisely the details which they narrated a year later at home. They could never forget the "headland which extended out there." This headland was, as the saga makes clear, one which B. L. Hadley, Acadia Park superintendent, described to the author as a "small isolated mountain which is called the 'flying mountain,' the Indian tradition being that this piece flew off from the larger mountain near it, and alighted in the sound." Less than half a mile from the entrance to Somes Sound, on its western side, and two hundred yards north of what became known centuries later as Jesuit Field, there is a spot that fits the description of Thorvald's first landing. It lies at the foot of tree-covered Flying Mountain, where the tumble of granite blocks shelves off steeply into deep water. This is the only place where the vikings would have found it possible to berth their ship, or, in the saga's words, "put out the gangplank to the shore."

Thorvald had of course left the afterboat at Leif's Shelters for the use of the men who were guarding the camp there. The ship carried only the two-man skiff, which could take only one man ashore with each round trip. A deep-water berthing place was as welcome as it was extraordinary.

Although the ocean level a thousand years ago was about two and one-half feet higher than at present, the state geologist of Maine may have been correct in saying that no considerable change in sea level in relation to the shore line on the Maine coast has occurred since the year of Thorvald's visit. The rise of ocean level and the postglacial uplift of land on the Maine coast may cancel each other. But even if the tidal levels in Somes Sound varied several feet from what they are now, the berthing place was unaffected, for there is a tide of twelve feet in Somes Sound. At whatever level of tide Thorvald berthed his ship, the shelving of the rocks into deep water made berthing possible, but only at a spot about a hundred feet in length. South of this, all the way to Jesuit Field, the water near shore is too shallow for berthing a viking ship, and from this spot all the way to the north end of Flying Mountain, the shore is a palisade too precipitous for landing. We can be very certain as to where the ship was berthed and Thorvald stepped ashore.

When Thorvald and his men stepped off the gangplank,

there was only one direction in which they could walk. They could not go north, where the granite shelf immediately steepens to a vertical cliff. They could not go to the westward up the sheer face of the mountainside. They could go only southward, along the widening shelf of rocks that becomes a flat shore of pebbles. Their ship was berthed at the end of a cul-de-sac. Since no one from the land could approach their ship except along the shore where they were going, they "all" dared leave the ship. It was like leaving a ship at one end of a long wharf with themselves at the landward end.

In going "up" on the land, they had to climb a fifteen-foot bank from the shore to the north end of Jesuit Field. *Thorvald then remarked: "Here it is fair, and here I should like to set up my residence."*

He was attracted to Jesuit Field because of the long vista into Somes Sound and the juxtaposition of mountains and sea. He immediately perceived the advantages of a site where a forested slope touched salt water, as it did all along the 200 yards of shore where he had walked. Above the shore, only a few feet from the water, grew timber, marketable with great profit in treeless Greenland, timber which could be rolled down the mountainside to the shore. Nowhere else had he found a site where the loading of a ship would be so easy.

When Thorvald stepped upon Jesuit Field, it was cleared land. (When the Jesuits came in 1613, the field had been cleared by centuries of Indian use.) If not entirely cleared for agriculture, most had been cleared by campers who cut down trees for firewood and left ancient shell heaps where they feasted.

Although it is impossible to be certain, the Indians of Somes Sound probably had customs similar to those of the Abenakis who lived on Mount Desert Island in post-Columbian times. In Thorvald's time, members of the Penobscot tribe related to the Algonquins summered on the island. George B. Street, in a history of Mount Desert, tells us that the Indians killed forest trees by girdling, to admit light to the soil where they planted maize and pumpkins and beans.

"These Penobscots . . . were regular visitors at Mount Desert, coming down each spring in their canoes, . . . digging clams, catching fish, trapping beaver, and then returning to . . . the Penobscot for the winter."

Thorvald saw quickly how ideal Jesuit Field would be for cattle. There was only one gap at the south end of the mountain through which cattle could escape, and if a fence only 200 feet long were erected there, cattle would be completely enclosed by water and mountain. The field, which had copious spring water, comprised twenty-five acres of gentle sloping and level land between the shore and the base of Flying Mountain. Thorvald had no difficulty in imagining a farmstead in this setting.

The particular spot where Thorvald wanted to build his dream house was probably near the middle of the tree-flanked western edge of Jesuit Field on the height there which commands the widest view. (There is now a large house on the site.)

They went afterward to the ship, and on the sands within the headland saw three mounds. They drew close and perceived there were three skin boats and three men under each. Then they divided their party and seized them all but one, who escaped with his boat. They killed those eight men.

Returning to the ship, Thorvald and his men sailed farther into the fjord along the base of the cliff, and as they came abreast of the north end of Flying Mountain, they began to see the impressive 690-foot rock wall, the sheer precipice of St. Sauveur Mountain, formerly called Dog Mountain. All eyes turned, as eyes now turn from every boat that sails into Somes Sound, to see what sort of bay or cove lay around on the west of Flying Mountain. Thorvald and his men, rounding the point, suddenly saw inside the cove the tiny sand beach about 150 yards from them, and three mounds upon it. Silently they steered toward these "sands within the headland" and as they drew close, they perceived that these mounds were upturned boats with three natives asleep under each.

The actual spot where the Indians lay is a sandy beach only fifty feet broad. On that small stretch of sand in Valley Cove occurred a historic event—the first recorded meeting between Europeans and American Indians.

Thorvald had left at least ten men at Leif's Shelters. He had at most twenty with him on the ship. Three or four remained on board to handle the ship, while the others, at most sixteen men, quietly slipped waist-deep into the water. Some went overboard just before the ship passed the sands and the others just after it passed, and they closed in on the sleeping Indians from both sides. The Indians got one of the canoes afloat. At least one man managed to escape. But the others were seized. The vikings had their hands full with eight captives. It probably never entered their minds that they might let the captives go. In the melee some blows had no doubt been struck by the Indians and the men's anger had been roused. And so they killed the eight Indians.

Thorvald and his men apparently did not immediately examine the material of which the two boats in their temporary possession were made, and they never had another opportunity to examine it. This is why they made what was probably an erroneous assumption that the covering of the two boats was animal skin, like the covering of Eskimo boats. The Indian boats in Valley Cove were more probably canoes of birch bark.

A variant version of the story in *Hauksbok* tells of a one-legged man "who skipped down to the shore" and disappeared. Possibly the mythological notion that unknown regions were inhabited by one-legged men, or unipeds, influenced that version, or possibly the Indian who escaped was wounded in one leg, and so helped shape the story. In any case, the vikings later said that a mountainous land north of Leif's Shelters was Uniped Land.

The *Flateyjarbok* continues Thorvald's adventures, or misadventures, this way:

Thereafter they ascended the headland and looked about, and saw within [up] the fjord some little hillocks, and sur-

mised that these were human habitations. Thereafter such great weariness befell them that they could not keep awake, and all fell asleep. Then came a call above them, such that they all awakened. This is what the call said: "Awake, Thou, Thorvald, and all Thy men, if Thou wouldst save Thy life, and go to Thy ship, Thou and all Thy men, and get clear of the land with all speed!" Then from the inner reaches of the fjord, countless skin boats were coming.

In less than a quarter of an hour, Thorvald and his men reached the summit of Flying Mountain, a natural lookout post, 284 feet in altitude. They probably followed an Indian trail up from Valley Cove, climbing a steepening slope under evergreens without underbrush for two thirds of the way and then over broken rock outcroppings the rest of the way.

From an open ledge at the south end of the summit they could see all the islands at the mouths of Somes Sound and the water approaches. From any of several ledges at the north end of the top of the narrow mountain they could see nearly all of Somes Sound, except what is concealed by the side of Acadia Mountain.

By the time Thorvald and his men reached these ledges, the escaped Indian had no doubt got out of sight behind Acadia Mountain. However, near the head of the fjord, three and three-quarter miles away from them, at a distance that made identification uncertain, Thorvald and his men saw a number of objects like little hillocks, which they "surmised" to be human habitations. These were actually Indian tepees, from which they may have seen smoke rising. The site of the principal Indian encampment in Somes Sound was visible from the summit of Flying Mountain just clear of the sloping edge of Acadia Mountain.

The unaccustomed climbing on a hot day had made Thorvald and his men as sleepy as the Indians had been. When they returned to the inviting shade of the woods close to the shore in the cove, they rested. Knowing that one of the natives had escaped, the vikings must have appointed one person to stay on guard. It seems certain that at least one watcher was posted on the ship, or close to it, on the point of land at the eastern end of Valley Cove, where there was deep water for the ship close to the rocks. But even if "all fell asleep," including the watcher, one man woke up in time to see the approaching peril and to warn the others.

The sound of the warning call appeared to come not from the ship or from the point of land at the east end of the cove, but from far above them. Local residents today have a second name for Valley Cove. They call it Echo Cove, and visitors entertain themselves with awakening the echoes from the rock wall of St. Sauveur Mountain.

When the warning outcry awakened Thorvald and his men, they saw with startled eyes the whole tribe of Indians who had been encamped at the side of a cove at the northern end of Somes Sound coming at them in canoes from around the base of Acadia Mountain. If question later arose as to which one had awakened them, each might have answered that he called a warning to others after he heard someone else yell. The unimportance of the question is implied by the impersonality with which the saga records the outcry. "Awake, Thou, Thorvald, and all Thy men, if Thou wouldst save Thy life. . . ." The warning cry was given with the formal "Thou" because it came from a man who, even in the emergency, was respectful to his leader, and was conscious that he was issuing a command that normally would have come from the lips of Thorvald.

The swift canoes of the war party when first spotted were less than a mile from the ship. This gave the vikings about eight minutes before the battle would be joined. Thorvald and his men had just enough time to scramble across a hundred yards of shore boulders to their ship, to row it away from shore, and to prepare themselves for defense as Thorvald ordered.

The skin boats made at them. Then Thorvald ordered: "We will put outboards the shields [mount the shields outside the gunwale] and defend ourselves as best we may, but attack only a little." So they did, and the Skraelings shot at them for a time, and then afterward fled, all as fast as they could. Then Thorvald asked his men whether they were in any way wounded, and they replied, "None wounded." "I have received a wound in my armpit," he said. "An arrow flew between the side of the ship and the shield and under my arm, and here is the arrow. If this leads to my death, I advise you to prepare to sail as soon as possible on your return passage, but carry me to that headland which seemed to me most habitable. It may be that a true word came out of my mouth, when I said I might dwell there for a while. There you shall bury me and set a cross at my head and at my feet, and call it Krossanes [Cross Cape] forever after." Now died Thorvald. They did everything that he told them to do, and then they went to rejoin their comrades, and they exchanged such tidings as they had, and they dwelt there that winter and gathered grapes, and vinestems for their ship. They prepared next spring to return to Greenland, and their ship came into Eriksfjörd and they had much to tell to Leif.

The rock wall of St. Sauveur Mountain echoed war whoops of avenging Indians who circled the ship in their canoes and shot their arrows at the vikings. If they attempted to board the ship, the three feet of freeboard supplemented by the storm shields made a five-foot rampart behind which Thorvald's men were successful in repelling them. The Indians fled when they had shot all their arrows, and perhaps had suffered casualties from swords wielded by the strong-armed, desperate defenders of the ship. Thus ended the first recorded battle between Europeans and American Indians. Dredging of the bottom of Valley Cove should bring up many Indian arrowheads.[1]

[1] It would be interesting to see if arrowheads from Valley Cove are of the same type as the arrowhead of Indian origin uncovered in the graveyard of the farm of Sandnes in Greenland, which belonged to Thorstein, the brother of Thorvald. That arrowhead, which may be the one that killed Thorvald, is in the Copenhagen Museum.

Thorvald, as leader, stood partly exposed with his arm holding the rudder, and retribution for the lives of the massacred Indians was swift. It must have been at least two or three o'clock in the afternoon when the men heard their leader say, "I have received a wound in my armpit." Thorvald obviously had not been struck in the heart, since he did not die at once. The arrow may have pierced his lung, his death resulting within a half hour.

Thorvald had counseled his men to sail away out of the fjord as soon as possible, but they had first to fulfill his dying wishes. They berthed the ship again, and some of them, bunched together to screen from prying enemy eyes what they were carrying, bore their leader's body from the ship to the burial place. They dug a grave deep enough to protect his remains from the depredations of animals; perhaps they concealed the grave under pine needles back in the woods. The grave would not have been deeper than thirty inches; for at the three-foot level in Jesuit Field there is hard clay very resistant to the pickax, and Thorvald's men did not have time before dark to dig a deeper grave than that. The crosses were probably not wooden stakes that would attract attention, but unobtrusive scratches or chiseled grooves on boulders. Unless the Indians found it, Thorvald's grave has remained undisturbed through the centuries. His brother Thorstein failed to recover the body, and the saga would have recorded any subsequent recovery of it by the vikings.

As described in the saga, the fjord where Thorvald Erikson met his death resembles in every respect Somes Sound in Mount Desert Island, the only fjord in New England. The points of identification are unmistakable, and there are too many for coincidence. We must conclude that the first Christian burial in North America took place in Somes Sound. Flying Mountain, which extends out at the entrance to Somes Sound, is the headland which Thorvald's men named Cross Cape.

Thorstein Erikson in Eriksfjörd had married Gudrid, Thorbiorn's daughter, who had been the wife of Thorer the

Eastman. Now Thorstein desired to go to Vinland for the body of his brother, and he fitted out the same ship and selected a crew of twenty-five strong and tall men. With Gudrid his wife he set out to sea, and out of land sight. They were driven this way and that all summer, and lost all reckoning of their whereabouts, but at the end of the first week of winter (mid-October), they came to land at Lysufirth in the Western Settlement of Greenland. There Thorstein found homes for all his crew, but not for himself and his wife, and the two of them spent two nights on the ship. Christianity at that time was young in Greenland. Then one called Thorstein the Swarthy invited them to his home, and he brought horses to fetch them to it, and he treated them well. Gudrid was a sturdy woman, and an understanding one who knew well how to behave among strangers. Early in the winter sickness came and many of Thorstein Erikson's men died. Thorstein the Swarthy ordered coffins made for the bodies, and had them carried to the ship to keep them there, "for I will take all the corpses to Eriksfjörd next summer." (Burials in frozen soil under deep snows were impossible in winter.) It was not long before sickness came to Thorstein the Swarthy's home, and his wife Grimhild was first taken ill, and then Thorstein Erikson. (Both died. Assumed to be dead before they really were, their "corpses" moved and spoke, and superstition had the "dead" Thorstein Erikson foretell the future career of his widow Gudrid.) In the spring, Thorstein the Swarthy sold his land and livestock and took ship with Gudrid and all his goods and sailed to Eriksfjörd, and dwelt there the rest of his days, and was considered to be a most honorable man.

13

Thorfinn Karlsefni's Vinland

Thorvald Erikson's explorations had extended viking knowledge of the coastline of Vinland to more than 500 miles. Thorfinn Karlsefni, an Icelander, soon extended that knowledge much farther. The *Flateyjarbok* again is our source.

That summer [1009] there arrived in Greenland from Norway a ship whose skipper was Thorfinn Karlsefni, son of Thord Horsehead, son of Snorre, son of Thor. Thorfinn Karlsefni was a man of great wealth in goods, and he spent the winter with Leif Erikson at Brattahlid, where he soon fell in love with Gudrid. When he asked for her hand, she referred him to Leif for her answer. They were betrothed and married that winter. At the same time there was again talk of a voyage to Vinland. Gudrid and others urged Karlsefni to attempt one. He decided in favor of the undertaking, and he hired ship-soldiers, sixty men, and five women, entering into an agreement that each one should have an equal share in any wealth acquired by the colony, for they intended to settle in the country if they had the power to do it. For that reason they carried with them all kinds of domestic animals. Karlsefni asked Leif for his buildings in Vinland, but Leif said he would lend them, not give them.

They put to sea and arrived safely at Leif's Shelters and carried up their leather bags. Soon they had plenty of good food, for a large and excellent whale was driven ashore, and they went to where it was and cut into it, and so had no shortage. The domestic animals were turned out to grass, but the

When the Norsemen first came to Iceland, Irish hermits who were living there went away. Later some missionary monks came from Ireland, and Christianity slowly took root. In this tapestry, from about the year 1400, St. Thorlák, a much-loved bishop of the twelfth century, is shown with his altar assistant.

This famous map establishes further evidence that the vikings had sailed to the World. It is believed to have been copied in about 1440 from an earlier source

ws "Vinland" in the upper left corner, west of Greenland. Above "Vinland" is
tin inscription, telling that "Bjarni and Leif Erikson discovered a new land."

Olaus Magnus, *Historia de Gentibus Septentrionalibus* (Rome, 1555). The New York Public Library, Rare Book Division.

Olaus Magnus, who was archbishop of Uppsala in the sixteenth century, wrote about the horrible sea monsters waiting to drown even the strongest sailors in the stoutest of ships. The vikings, however, who were much more knowledgeable about the sea, provided detailed sailing directions to navigators of the North Atlantic.

Olaus Magnus, *Historia de Gentibus Septentrionalibus* (Rome, 1555). The New York Public Library, Rare Book Division

When Leif Erikson died (c.1025), the morale of the Greenlanders died too. Life was hard, and after years of poor diet and intermarriage with encroaching Eskimos, they were no longer a tall and stalwart race. This fanciful medieval drawing shows Greenland pigmies advancing on a group of birds larger than they are.

Christianity was forced on Norway by Olaf Tryggvason in the tenth century. Somewhat earlier, Denmark was converted by Harald Bluetooth, whose tombstone at Jelling (right) bears the oldest picture of Christ in the north countries.

Viking art. Left—stone carving from Uppland, Sweden, showing horse not much bigger than its rider. Right—bronze statuette of Thor, god of thunder, from Iceland.

After Karlsefni had decided that Vinland could not be colonized, expeditions to the new land decreased and eventually stopped. By about 1075 the viking period was over, not only in Vinland, but in Europe too. In this ninth-century illumination, Norsemen go aboard their ships as they leave England.

After three years in Vinland, Karlsefni's colonists gave up and went home to Greenland. Battle-axes used to fight the Indians no doubt looked something like this one, which was dug up from a viking chieftain's grave in Mammen, Jutland.

Photo by Albert F. Haas; The Rhode Island Historical Society

This stone tower above the harbor of Newport, Rhode Island, was probably built in the thirteenth or fourteenth century by descendants of the vikings.

This viking sword was found in 1911 near Ulen, Minnesota, adding to the evidence that Norsemen did explore the area.

John L. Denison, *Die illustrierte neue Welt* (1858). Library of Congress

One of Leif's crew, a German called Tyrker, found grapes on Cape Cod. For the grapes, and for the greenbrier vines, Leif named the country "Vinland."

John L. Denison, *Die illustrierte neue Welt* (1858). Library of Congress

Karlsefni married Leif's sister-in-law Gudrid. He took her, along with other prospective colonists, to Leif's Shelters at Follins Pond. There Indians came out of the forest to trade their animal skins for cow's milk.

males soon became very frisky and wild. They had brought one bull with them. Karlsefni had trees cut down and shaped into timbers to make a shipload, and this wood was stacked upon a rock for drying. They gathered a supply of all the good things which the country produced, wineberries and game and fish.

During the summer following their first winter, they became aware of the presence of the Skraelings, a great band of whom came out of the forest. The cattle were near at hand and the bull bellowed and roared mightily. This frightened the Skraelings who fled with their bundles. But those were gray fur and sable and all kinds of skinwares, and they turned toward Karlsefni's abode and tried to enter the buildings. Karlsefni and his men held the doors to keep them out. Neither side understood the language of the other. Then the Skraelings put down their packs and loosened them and offered their wares in trade, showing especial eagerness for weapons. Karlsefni forbade his companions to trade any weapons, but got the idea of having the women carry milk out to them. The moment they saw the milk, they wanted it, and nothing else. Thus the conclusion of the Skraelings' trading was that they carried their goods away in their stomachs, while they left their bundles and fur skins with Karlsefni and his men.

Following this occurrence, Karlsefni had a strong fence of palings erected around his abode and made all ready there. At this time Gudrid his wife gave birth to a male child, who was called Snorre.

Early in the second winter the Skraelings came again, in larger numbers, with the same wares as before. Karlsefni then told the women to trade milk as they had before, and nothing else. When the Skraelings saw the milk, they threw their bundles in over the palisade. While Gudrid was seated inside the doorway beside the cradle of her infant son, Snorre, a shadow fell upon the door and a woman in a black narrow kirtle entered. She was a short woman, with a band about her head, and light chestnut hair, and pale skin, and such large eyes as had never been seen in a human head.

The woman went to where Gudrid sat and asked: "What is thy name?"

"My name is Gudrid; but what is thy name?"

"My name is Gudrid," said the woman. The housewife, Gudrid, pointed with her hand to a seat beside her, but at that instant there was a great crash, and the woman disappeared. One of the Skraelings who had tried to seize some weapons had been slain by one of Karlsefni's men, and instantly they fled, leaving garments and goods behind them. No one save Gudrid had seen the woman.

Now we shall have to plan against them," said Karlsefni, "for I think they will return a third time to attack us in great force. This is what we shall do. Let ten of our men go out upon this cape and show themselves, while the rest of us will slip into the woods and hew a clearing for our cattle, when the savages advance from the forest. We shall take our bull also and let him precede us."

The site chosen for the battlefield lay between water and forest. Karlsefni's strategy worked. The Skraelings advanced to the chosen battle site. In the fight many Skraelings were killed. Among them was a tall and fair man who Karlsefni believed was their chieftain. One of the Skraelings picked up an ax and examined it. Then he lifted it against his comrade and struck at him, and he was instantly felled. At this the tall man seized the ax, and after looking at it for a while, hurled it with all his might out into the salt water. Then they all fled into the forest. Thus the battle ended.

Karlsefni stayed there throughout the winter, but in the spring decided to remain no longer, but return to Greenland. They made ready for the voyage and took with them great quantities of berries, and skinwares. They set sail upon the open ocean and arrived safely at Eriksfjörd, where they spent the following winter.

In planning the expedition, Karlsefni and his followers had agreed to establish a colony in Vinland "if they had the power to do it [*ef their metti that*]." This shows that the story of the many Skraelings who had joined battle against Thorvald's ship made the vikings temper their purpose with an if. They were uncertain whether their numbers would be sufficient to maintain a settlement against a large population of hostile natives.

The *Flateyjarbok* omits all details of the voyage to Leif's campsite. It does not tell how many ships took part in Karlsefni's expedition. Without any hint to the contrary, it implies that Karlsefni remained at Leif's Shelters until he returned to Greenland. It concentrates on his experiences at Leif's Shelters, but about his explorations of continental Vinland before and after he arrived there, it says absolutely nothing. One may suspect, therefore, that the Greenlanders who were, it is believed, the source of the *Flateyjarbok* story, from a too-narrow loyalty to Leif Erikson's family, deliberately omitted the achievements of Thorfinn Karlsefni.

The *Hauksbok* narrative, on the other hand, which emanated from descendants of Karlsefni in Iceland, never even mentions Leif's Shelters, or any of Karlsefni's experiences at Leif's Shelters, but it does tell the full story of Karlsefni's explorations. Its comment on the Yule feast that Leif Erikson provided at Brattahlid—"about the most magnificent ever seen there"—expresses the scorn Icelanders felt for the best Leif Erikson could offer and their condescension toward the comparative poverty of Greenlanders. The *Hauksbok* steps aside from its central theme to relate the moving story of a fellow Icelander, Bjarni Grimolfsson, and to picture his self-sacrifice in its heroic proportions. The following pages are translated from *Hauksbok*:

Thorfinn Karlsefni was a prosperous merchant who had made various trading voyages. One summer he fitted out his ship to sail to Greenland. Snorri Thorbrandsson of Alptafirth in Iceland and forty other men were with him. Bjarni Grimolfsson from Breidafirth and Thorhall Gamlinsson from Eastfirth, also with forty men, fitted out their ship the same

summer for the same purpose. The two ships put to sea together and both arrived at Eriksfjörd in the autumn. The inhabitants of the country rode to the ships and there was much
good trading. Gudrid was invited by the owners of the ships
to help herself to whatever of their wares she desired, and
Erik [a mistake for Leif Erikson], not to be outdone in generosity, offered the hospitality of winter quarters for both
crews at Brattahlid. The cargoes were carried to Brattahlid,
where there were warehouses of sufficient size, and the merchants were well cared for and pleasurably entertained
throughout the winter. Great preparations were made for the
Yule feast, which was about the most magnificent ever seen
there. After Yule, Karlsefni, who had fallen in love with Gudrid, asked for her hand in marriage. She referred him to Leif
for her answer, through whom they were formally betrothed,
and that same winter their bridal was drunk.

And now at Brattahlid there was much talk of exploration of Vinland the Good, for men said that land must have
many good qualities. Thus it came about that Karlsefni and
Snorri and their crew prepared to sail in search of Vinland
in the spring. Bjarni and Thorhall [Thorhall Gamlinsson,
not Thorhall the Huntsman] and their crew decided to accompany them with the other ship.

Bjarni Grimolfsson and his shipmates were driven out
into the Irish Ocean [the Atlantic between Ireland and New-
foundland], and their ship became infested with worms, and
before they knew, it was all worm-eaten beneath them and
began to sink. They had an afterboat which had been protected with seal tar so that the teredo worms would not attack it. They began to take their places in this boat, but found
that it would not hold more than half their number. Then
said Bjarni: "The men who are to go in the boat should be
chosen by lot, not by rank." This appealed to everyone as
being such a manly offer that no one said nay to it. They
adopted this plan and drew lots, and Bjarni was thus chosen
to go into the boat with half of the men, but when they were
settled in the boat and about to cast off, a young Icelander

who had remained in the ship and who had come out from Iceland with Bjarni, said: "Bjarni, are you going to leave me here?"

"It must be," Bjarni answered.

"That is not what you promised my father when I left Iceland with you. You told him that we should share the same fate."

"So be it," said Bjarni. "We will exchange places. You come into the boat and I will go to the ship; for I see you are eager to live."

Bjarni then boarded the ship and the boy took his place in the boat, and the boat sailed away until they came to Dublin in Ireland and there they told this tale. It is generally believed that Bjarni and his men were drowned in the worm-infested sea, for they were never heard of again.

Karlsefni sailed first to the Western Settlement and from there to Bear Island [Disco Island (?) at 70° North], and thence across the open sea to the southward for two days' sailing distance, and saw land [southern tip of Cumberland Peninsula of Baffin Land]. They put over a boat and explored the country and found large flat rocks there, many of them twelve ells [twenty-seven feet] in width, and many Arctic foxes. They called this country Helluland. They then sailed with northerly winds for two days' sailing distance, and then land lay ahead [northern tip of Labrador], and it was well wooded, with many wild animals. There was an island [Newfoundland] off to the southeast of this land, and because they found a bear there they called it Bear Island [Biarney], while they called the wooded land Markland. From there they sailed southward along the land for a long time, and came to a cape. The land was off to the starboard, with long beaches and sand dunes. They rowed ashore and found on the cape the keel of a ship, and thereafter called it Keel Cape. They called the beaches Wonder-strands [Furdustrandir], because they were so long to sail by. Beyond these Wonder-strands, the country was indented with bays, into one of which they sailed.

This is all *Hauksbok* tells of Karlsefni's entering Nantucket Sound, and so it avoids any mention of Leif's Shelters.

As expressed in *Hauksbok*, Karlsefni's purpose was much larger than to attempt to establish a colony in Vinland. It was to sail "in search of Vinland." This phrase has a broader significance than any other in all the narratives of the Vinland voyages. Why would the saga say that Karlsefni at Brattahlid desired to "sail in search" of a land to which the sailing directions were perfectly well known and had in fact been given to him by his host who had been to that land? Moreover, that land had been visited by a number of the men who were at Brattahlid, and its coast had been explored for 500 miles by a previous expedition led by the brother of his host. The word "search" would not have been used if it had been Karlsefni's intention to sail from Brattahlid directly to Leif's Shelters. "In search of Vinland" did not apply to getting to Leif's Shelters, but meant a search to determine the full extent of the land called Vinland, which Thorvald Erikson's explorations had showed to be a huge country. The words "in search of" meant "to explore."

Wherever they could, viking explorers avoided duplicating the voyages previous vikings had made. The details of Karlsefni's route from Brattahlid are revealing and were geographically well reasoned. Men in the Western Settlement of Greenland had of course sighted land, Baffin Land, about two days' sailing distance to the west of them. Karlsefni, with a tremendous breadth of vision, saw the geographical possibilities of sailing not southwest to Leif's Shelters but northwest to the Western Settlement. He planned then to cross to the land to the west and to follow the coast of that land southward to see whether it was continuous with the coast of Thorvald Erikson's Vinland. Accordingly, he turned the prow of his ship first north and then west. The other ships bearing prospective Vinland colonists probably sailed from Brattahlid directly to an appointed rendezvous in Vinland. Karlsefni had no doubt learned at Brattahlid that the land at Leif's campsite was very sandy, and that better land for agriculture lay beyond Leif's Shelters to the west.

Karlsefni found the land to the west of the Western Settlement was not continuous with Vinland. At least he assumed it was not, since he had to cross open sea for two days southward to the northern tip of another land, Labrador. He gave Labrador the name Leif Erikson had previously and for the same reason given to Newfoundland. Karlsefni found that the coast of Labrador led into a well-wooded region, the Gulf of St. Lawrence, where there was an island, Newfoundland, "off to the southeast of this land." In further following of the coast he came to the tall-forested Markland, where men on his ship, recognizing the Markland coast from previous voyages with Leif and Thorvald Erikson, must have told him that he was now in the pattern of the old sailing directions. Nevertheless, he apparently did not follow these sailing directions, for *Hauksbok* specifically says he "sailed southward along the land for a long time, and came to a cape" where he found an abandoned ship's keel. We recognize that he had reached Thorvald Erikson's Keel Cape, Cape Cod. The overall direction was "southward," but following the coast involved at least one day's sailing northward around the western end of Nova Scotia into the Bay of Fundy. This satisfied him that the coast of Markland was continuous with that of New Brunswick and Maine. From there he followed the coast to Keel Cape. Either on this outward voyage or later "with one ship" Karlsefni perceived that Markland was part of great Vinland.

Thus far, Karlsefni had established that the coast of Vinland was continuous from the northern tip of Labrador to Cape Cod. The *Hauksbok* narrative continues with Karlsefni's explorations beyond Leif's Shelters.[1]

When Leif had visited King Olaf Tryggvason, the king had given him two Gaels [Irishmen], advising him to make use of them if speed was ever required, for they could run faster than deer. Of these two, the man's name was Haki and the woman's Haekia. Leif had loaned this couple to Karlsefni,

---

[1] For geographical identifications see my books *The Lost Discovery*, pp. 161–66, and *Atlantic Crossings Before Columbus*, p. 151.

and when Karlsefni's party had sailed past Wonder-strands, they set the Gaels on shore and ordered them to run to the southward to scout out the nature of the land, and to return before the end of the third half day.

The Gaels when set ashore were attired in a garment called kiafal, open at the sides and sleeveless, with a hood at the top, and held between the legs with buttons and loops. Except for this they were naked. Karlsefni's people lay at anchor while they were gone, and when the Gaels returned, one of them had a bunch of wineberries, and the other an ear of a new kind of cultivated wheat [hveitiax nýsáit]. After the Gaels got on board, Karlsefni and his crew sailed along until they came to where the coast was indented with bays. They sailed their ship into a bay at the mouth of which was an island in the midst of strong currents, for which reason they called it Stream Island [Straumey]. There were so many birds there, it was barely possible to step between the eggs. They sailed through the fjord and called it Stream Fjord, and transported their goods from the ship to the shore, and set up camp. They had brought with them all kinds of live-stock, and it was a splendid country there. There were mountains thereabouts. They did nothing except to explore the country. They remained there during the winter.

The variant text in the Arnamagnaean Library (A.M. 557) here continues the story:

They had taken no thought for provisions during the summer. The fishing began to fail, and they began to fall short of food.

Then Thorhall the Huntsman disappeared. They had already prayed to God for food, but it did not come as promptly as their necessities seemed to demand. They searched for Thorhall for three half days, and found him on a pro-jecting crag. He was lying there looking up at the sky, with mouth and nostrils agape, and mumbling something. They asked him why he had gone thither; he replied that it was nobody's business. They asked him then to go home [to the camp] with them, and he did so. Soon after this a whale appeared there [New York Harbor, not in the northern Hudson], and they captured it, and flensed it, and no one could tell what manner of whale it was, and when the cooks had prepared it they ate of it, and were all made ill by it. Then Thorhall, approaching them, said: "Did not the Red-beard [the god Thor] prove more helpful than your Christ? This is my reward for the verses which I composed to Thor, the Trustworthy; seldom has he failed me." When the people heard this they cast the whale down into the sea, and made their appeals to God. The weather then improved, and they could now row out to fish, and thenceforward they had no lack of provisions, for they could hunt game on the land, gather eggs on the island, and catch fish from the sea.

It is said that Thorhall wished to sail to the northward beyond Wonder-strands in search for Wineland, while Karlsefni desired to proceed to the southward, off the coast. Thorhall prepared for his voyage out below the island, having only nine men in his party, for all the remainder of the company went with Karlsefni. And one day when Thorhall was carrying water aboard his ship, he recited this ditty:

> When I came, these brave men told me,
>   Here the best of drink I'd get.
> Now with water pail behold me,
>   Wine and I are strangers yet.
> Stooping at the spring I've tasted
>   All the wine this land affords;
> Of its vaunted charms divested,
>   Poor indeed are its rewards.

And when they were ready, they hoisted sail; whereupon Thorhall recited this ditty:

> Comrades, let us now be faring
>   Homeward to our own again!
> Let us try the sea-steed's daring,

Give the chafing courser rein.
Those who will may bide in quiet,
Let them praise this chosen land,
Feasting on a whale-steak diet,
In their home by Wonder-strand.

Then they sailed away to the northward past Wonder-
strands and Keel Cape, intending to cruise to the westward
around the cape. They encountered westerly gales, were
driven ashore in Ireland, where they were grievously mal-
treated and thrown into slavery. There Thorhall lost his life,
according to that which traders have related.

The narrative continues in the Hauksbok:

It is said that Karlsefni sailed southward along the coast
with Snorri and their people. They sailed for a long time
and went on until they came all the way to where there was a
river that flowed down from the land to wide water, thence
to the sea. There were great sand banks, [tongues of land running into the sea], and one could enter only at flood. There
Karlsefni entered in, and called it Hóp. In that country they
found fields of self-sown wheat in the lowlands, and vines on
the hills. Every brook there was full of fish. They dug pits
on the flats where the tide rose highest, and when the tide
fell, holy fish were in the pits. A great many wild animals of
all sorts were in the woods. They remained there half a month
and enjoyed themselves, without keeping watch. They had
their livestock with them. Early one morning when they
looked out they saw a great many skin canoes, and staves
[paddles] being swung about on the boats with a noise like
flails, and they were being revolved in the direction in which
the sun moves. Then Karlsefni said: "What is the meaning
of this?" Snorri Thorbrandsson answered him: "Possibly this
is a peace signal, and so let us show them a white shield."
They did this, and the strangers rowed toward them and
stared with wonderment at those they saw before them, and
then came up on the land. They were swarthy and ill-looking

men, and had ugly hair on their heads. They had large eyes and broad cheeks. They stayed there for a while staring at those they saw before them, and then rowed away to the southward beyond the point.

Karlsefni's party had built their shelters above the lake, some near it and some farther off, and there they spent that winter. There came no snow at all and all of their livestock lived by grazing.

Early one morning in the spring they saw a great many skin canoes rowing around the point, looking like coals flung out beyond the bay, and staves being swung about on every boat. Then Karlsefni's men showed their shields, and they came together and began to trade, and those people especially wished red cloth, for which they exchanged fur skins and all-gray skins. They wished also to purchase swords and spears, but Karlsefni and Snorri refused them. In return for unblemished skins, the savages would accept a span length of red cloth and bind it around their heads. Thus the trading continued. When Karlsefni's people began to run short of cloth, they ripped it into pieces so narrow that none were broader than a finger, but the savages even then gave as much for it as before, or more. This continued until a bull of Karlsefni's ran out of the woods bellowing loudly. This terrified the savages so that they ran out to their boats and rowed away southward along the shore.

Nothing was seen of them for three weeks, but at the end of that time, such a great number of the boats of the savages appeared that they looked like a floating stream, and their staves were all revolving in a direction opposite to the course of the sun, and they were all whooping with great outcries. Then Karlsefni's men took red shields and held them up to view. The savages leaped from their boats, and they met and fought. There was a heavy shower of missiles, for the savages had war slings. Karlsefni observed that the savages had on the end of a pole a great ball-shaped object almost the size of a sheep's belly, and nearly as black in color, and this they flung from the pole up on the land above Karlsefni's men, and it made such a terrifying noise where it struck the ground that great fear seized Karlsefni and all with him, so that they thought only of flight and of making their escape up along the riverbank. It seemed to them that the savages were driving at them from all sides, and they did not make a stand until they came to a certain cliff where they resisted fiercely.

Freydis came out and seeing that Karlsefni and his men were retreating, called out: "Why run from these wretched creatures, such worthy men as you are? It looks to me as though you might slaughter them like cattle. If I had a weapon, I believe I would fight better than any of you!" They heeded her not. Freydis wanted to join them, but fell behind, for she was pregnant. She followed them, nevertheless, into the woods, the savages pursuing her. In front of her she found a dead man, Thorbrand Snorrason, whose skull had been split by a flat stone. His drawn sword lay beside him. She took it up and prepared to wield it in self-defense. Then the savages came at her, and she uncovered her breast and slapped it with the naked sword. This sight so terrified the savages that they ran down to their boats and paddled away. Karlsefni and his men joined her and praised her courage.

Only two of Karlsefni's men had been slain, but a great number of the savages, although Karlsefni's men had been outnumbered. They now returned to their shelters, and bound up their wounds, and discussed what sort of men that great host had been that had seemed to sweep down upon them from the land side. It was realized that there could have been but one host of savages, the one which came from the boats, and that the other had been a self-deception, an illusion.

The savages had found a dead man, and his ax lying beside him. They had taken up the ax and had struck at a tree, all and sundry trying it, and it seemed to them a treasure, for it bit well. Later on, one of them had taken it and had struck at a slab of rock so that the ax broke, and they thought it useless, since it would not split stone, and threw it away.

It now seemed obvious to Karlsefni's party that, although the surrounding country appeared attractive, they could live there only with fear and warfare, because of the natives. Accordingly, they prepared to depart, and decided to return to their own country. They sailed northward along the coast, and found five savages in skin doublets, asleep near the sea. They had dishes of animal marrow and blood beside them. Karlsefni's followers thought that these men had been exiled, and slew them. Afterward they found a cape where there were a great number of animals, and this cape appeared to be one cake of dung from the droppings of the animals which lay there at night. Now they came again to Stream Fjord, where they soon had plenty of all the things they needed.

Some men say that Gudrid remained here with ten times ten men and went no farther, and that Karlsefni and Snorri went farther south with forty men, but that they did not tarry at Hóp longer than two months and came back the same summer. While most of the men remained behind, Karlsefni with one ship sailed to the northward around Keel Cape and from there bore off to the westward [to keep in sight of the coast], with land on the larboard. As far as they could see, it was a forested wilderness there with almost nowhere an open space. After they had gone a great distance, there was a river that flowed down from the east to the west. They sailed into its mouth and lay to at its southern bank. Then they sailed away to the north and believed they were getting a glimpse of Uniped Land, but were unwilling to risk their lives any longer. They concluded that the mountains of Hóp and those which they now [probably while returning] found formed one mountain chain, and this seemed to be so since both sides were the same distance from Stream Fjord.

They spent the third winter at Stream Fjord. Then the men began to form factions because of the women, and those without wives sought to possess the wives of those who had them, and this caused the greatest trouble. The first autumn Snorre, the son of Karlsefni was born, and he was three winters old when they departed. When they sailed away from Vinland they had wind from the south and bore in upon Markland and found five savages there, one bearded, two women, and two children. Karlsefni seized the children, but the other savages got away and disappeared as though they had sunk into the earth. The two boys they took away with them, and taught them the language, and they were baptized. They said their mother's name was Vethilldi and their father's Evege. They said kings [tribal chiefs] ruled over the Skraelings, and that one of them was named Avalldama and another, Avilldudida, and that there were caves, but no houses, and the people there lived among the rocks or in holes. They said there lay a land over against their land [Newfoundland?], the inhabitants of which wore white clothes [priests] and carried poles before them festooned with rags [religious banners] and yelled loudly [chanted]. People believe this must have been White Man's Land or Great Ireland.

In the inland waters to the west of Leif's Shelters, Karlsefni chose to explore the north shore of Long Island. This choice strengthens our assumption that Thorvald Erikson's afterboat party, starting from the mouth of the Bass River, went westward along the south shore of Cape Cod, of Massachusetts in Buzzards Bay, of Rhode Island, and of Connecticut. If Thorvald's party had explored the north shore of Long Island, there would have been no reason for Karlsefni's doing it.

The north shore of Long Island is unique in several geographical particulars, and details in the *Hauksbok* identify it beyond question. It was an extensive shore which called for investigation "to the southward." The only extensive north shore beyond Keel Cape is the north shore of Long Island. The north shore of Long Island from Orient Point to Flushing Bay is about ninety miles, and the first half of it is a beach, unbroken except by a narrow creek at Mattituck and a narrower one at Wading River. This continuous forty-five miles of beach was the second Wonder-strand. Karlsefni's party sailed past the beach toward the first beckoning high ground close to the shore, the hill of 180 feet elevation between Mount Sinai Harbor and Port Jefferson Harbor. This

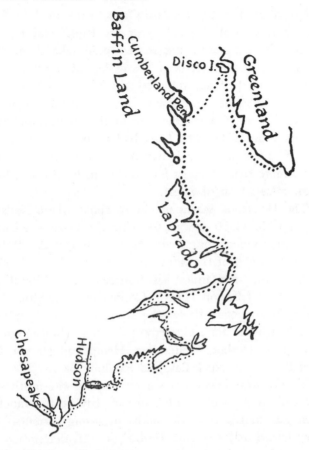

While still in Vinland, Karlsefni explored the North American coast. Rounding Long Island's north shore, he sailed up the fjord that is the Hudson River, and his party camped for the winter near Albany. The next summer he sailed down the coast as far as Chesapeake Bay.

high ground, Belle Terre, was visible to Karlsefni's lookout at mast height from twenty-five miles away. Since he was exploring, Karlsefni undoubtedly climbed this hill. From it he could see higher hills several miles to the south (232 feet altitude at South Setauket, and over 200 feet between Selden and

Farmingville). He sent the two Gaels to run to those higher hills "to scout out the nature of the land," and from the distances he reasonably judged it would take them "three half days." It must have been late in August or early September, for one of the Gaels returned with a bunch of wild grapes. The other brought some grain that was *nýsáit*—"new" and "sown." It was of a species new to the vikings, and it was cultivated, not wild. The Gael had robbed an Indian corn patch. The largest ear of Indian corn in the eleventh century was no more than three or four inches in length, and looked like an enlarged ear of wheat.

The *Hauksbok* leaves no doubt about where Karlsefni's party put the Gaels ashore, for after the Gaels got back on board, they "sailed along a coast that was indented with bays." The western half of the north shore of Long Island is a coast which in forty-five miles has fourteen bays: Mount Sinai Harbor, Port Jefferson Harbor, Conscience Bay, Stony Brook Harbor, Nissequogue River (the last two in great Smithtown Bay), Northport Bay, Centerport Harbor, Huntington Bay, Cold Spring Harbor, Oyster Bay, Hempstead Harbor, Manhasset Bay, Little Neck Bay, and Flushing Bay.

To the west beyond the many bays of the north shore, Karlsefni's party sailed into another "bay at the mouth of which was an island in the midst of strong currents." Governors Island in New York Harbor fits this description. The bay was also at the mouth of a "fjord"—the Hudson River. They sailed "through the fjord," past the Palisades and through the Highlands of the Hudson River, which they called Stream Fjord, and they found "mountains thereabouts." Karlsefni's party made camp for the winter somewhere north of the Highlands and probably north of the Catskill Mountains, near Albany, or slightly north of Albany at Waterford; it was the viking custom to penetrate a fjord or river to the limit of navigability.

In exploring the Hudson, Karlsefni's party had Snorri Thorbrandsson's and Thorhall's ships. While Snorri and the others remained in the winter camp, Karlsefni probably returned in his own ship to Leif's Shelters to spend the winter with his wife in Leif's house.

Will the campsite up the Hudson ever be found? Perhaps it has already been found in the ancient sites on a former island which is now incorporated into the river frontage at Albany. Those sites have never been explained. They were not Indian and they preceded the first Dutch settlement there. They may have been sixteenth-century French. A search, however, should be made at Waterford, at the actual limit of Hudson navigability.

Wherever the camp was, the river froze. Since the vikings could not fish, they almost starved. In earliest spring, as soon as the ice in the river broke, they sailed out of the fjord to the bay at its mouth, where they were able to fish and gather birds' eggs for food. Stream Fjord was obviously of considerable length, with winter very severe far inland and much warmer at its mouth.

The *Hauksbok* does not make clear where Karlsefni spent his winters in Vinland. "They spent the third winter at Stream Fjord" refers, I think, only to those men and women who remained there, while Karlsefni with his ship no doubt returned to Leif's Shelters to winter with his wife and infant son in a house protected by a palisade. The saga suggests that he did not take his wife with him everywhere he went exploring—"Some men say that Gudrid remained here [New York Harbor] with ten times ten men and went no farther." The sentence "Now it is said that Karlsefni sailed southward along the coast with Snorri Thorbrandsson and his people" seems to imply that Karlsefni had not wintered up the Hudson but had the next year joined Snorri's party for this coastal exploration. We may be sure that Karlsefni wintered wherever Gudrid was. The *Flateyjarbok* says he spent his winters at Leif's Shelters, and *Hauksbok* says Snorre, born the first autumn, was three winters old when they departed.

From New York Harbor, Karlsefni, who rejoined Snorri Thorbrandsson, sailed "southward along the coast . . . for a long time" and came to a bay which they called *Hóp*, meaning bay or inlet. Hóp was in all probability Chesapeake Bay. "A river flowed down from the land into wide water and thence into the sea." There Karlsefni's party "built their shelters above water, some near it and some farther off." A search should be made for foundations of house sites and at least one ship shed end on to the water up the river which best fits the description.

In the desperate battle at Hóp, Karlsefni saw the Skraelings fling from the end of a pole "a great ball-shaped object almost the size of a sheep's belly, and nearly as black in color," which "made such a terrifying noise where it struck the ground" that Karlsefni's men "thought only of flight." The saga afterward tells what in the heat of battle they had supposed the sound portended. William L. Smyth of Winsted, Connecticut, makes the acceptable suggestion that the weapon was a white-faced hornets' nest (*Vespa maculata*), which John C. Pallister of the Department of Entomology of the American Museum of Natural History says Indians did use in fighting. It was a formidable weapon that required most careful handling; for its walls were thin and fragile, like paper. The opening, normally at the bottom, could not be effectually sealed, and the only way the Indians could get control of it was at night to slip an animal skin up over the nest, which was the size of a football, or in some cases as large as a basketball. As they cut the nest free from the support from which it hung, they closed and tied the mouth of the animal skin. Thus the nest, which was slate gray in color, was inside a dark skin that would look black against the sky. When the Indians were ready to fling the nest with the spring of a pole, they would untie the mouth of the animal skin and let go the insect bomb. The terrifying noise "where" it struck the ground (not when, or just at the moment it struck, but afterward, beginning and growing louder and continuous) was the shrill stridulation of 3,000 to 4,000 hornets. Mistaking this sound for the war-whooping of another band of Skraelings on the high ground in back of them, Karlsefni and his men precipitately fled. One can outrun hornets, and if the Skraelings' weapon landed as far as forty feet away, none of the vikings got stung.

The action of Freydis in baring her breast and slapping it with the sword was a gesture of defiance familiar to vikings before a battle, and Freydis not only frightened the savages but shamed Karlsefni's men into renewed courage. Her gesture no doubt evoked some superstitious fear among the Skraelings. It may have appealed to the gallantry of the Indian men, for there have been cases recorded in which Indian women laid bare their bosoms, thus disclosing their sex, apparently with confidence that by so doing their lives would be spared by their enemies.[2]

It was probably beyond the imagination of the vikings to realize that they themselves had caused the warfare with the Indians. The sagas clearly show that the vikings disapproved of the Skraelings; they must have showed their disgust and fear in their faces. The Indians were too many for them, and after three years, Karlsefni abandoned the attempted settlement. His decision appears to have ended viking desires to settle in Vinland. Eventually, Vinland faded into a lost discovery, to be rediscovered in our time.

Karlsefni "with one ship" sailed to the northward around Keel Cape, and from there "bore off to the westward," crossing twenty-five miles from the north end of Cape Cod to the shore of Massachusetts Bay. Then "with land on the larboard," he sailed to the north. Later, sailing down east off the Maine coast, he probably had a following wind that made it convenient to cross the gap of the Bay of Fundy before investigating its shores in detail. He and his men came to a river unique among all they had found, in that it flowed down from the east to the west. This was undoubtedly Apple River in Nova Scotia. The mouth of Apple River is a mile wide, with a tidal basin three miles long. Present-day villages are all on the south side of Apple River, and Karlsefni's ship "lay to at its southern bank." From there they sailed away to the north

[2] James Patrick Howley, *The Beothucks or Red Indians: The Aboriginal Inhabitants of Newfoundland*, p. 261.

for twenty miles into Chignecto Bay, until Karlsefni had verified that Markland (Nova Scotia) was indeed part of Vinland. Following the coast on his return, they passed Mount Desert Island and believed they were now getting a glimpse of Uniped Land, where Thorvald Erikson had met his death, but they were unwilling to risk their lives in a close inspection. Thorvald's body had been in the grave five years.

Farther along on their return, Karlsefni sighted the Presidential Range in New Hampshire from off the Maine coast. They concluded that the mountains of *Hóp* and those which they now saw formed one mountain chain; for the saga tells us that the mountains of *Hóp* seen from the river they ascended inside the bay were the same distance away from the mountains at Stream Fjord as were the mountains they now saw to the north of Keel Cape. The distances, as the crow flies, are approximately the same from the Blue Ridge in Virginia to the Highlands of the Hudson, and from the Highlands of the Hudson to the Presidential Range in New Hampshire. Karlsefni had not only explored the seacoast and the rivers and bays, but he unquestionably discovered the Appalachian Mountains.

Karlsefni is also to be credited with having established that the coast of Vinland was continuous from the northern tip of Labrador (60° North) to the Chesapeake (37° North), and that Vinland was a country of continental size. In his "search," Karlsefni by the year 1012 personally had seen at least 2,500 miles of the coast line of North America. One of the world's great explorers, his accomplishment matches the work of John Cabot, who, according to his son Sebastian, in 1498 explored the coast from the northern tip of Labrador to the Chesapeake—"to the latitude of Gibraltar."

14

Freydis

Although Greenlanders gave up all hope of a permanent settlement in Vinland, they still dreamed of the wealth to be gained there. The vines and timber Leif and Thorvald's men had brought back were in great demand, and the furs Thorfinn brought commanded high prices in Europe. Erik's daughter Freydis coveted the wealth of these men.

When two Icelandic brothers Helgi and Finnbogi arrived with their ship at Eriksfjörd, Freydis saw her opportunity. She proposed that the brothers join her in an expedition to Vinland, sharing equally the profits. Her husband Thorvard, who apparently was a rather spineless character, accompanied his determined wife. But none of the party had any thought of settling in Vinland or of prolonging the stay beyond one winter. The *Flateyjarbok* is our source for the events of the expedition.

There was much new talk in Greenland about voyaging to Vinland, an enterprise now considered both profitable and honorable. The same summer that Karlsefni returned from Vinland, a ship arrived from Norway under the command of two brothers, Helgi and Finnbogi. They wintered in Greenland. These brothers were of Icelandic stock from the Eastfjords. Now it is to be told that Freydis, Erik's daughter, went forth from her home at Gardar to have a talk with the brothers Helgi and Finnbogi, and invited them to voyage in their ship to Vinland and to go halves with her on all the profit that might be obtained there. They agreed to this. She went thence to her brother Leif and asked him to give her the house he had built in Vinland. He gave her his former answer, that he would lend the house, not give it. It was agreed that each ship should carry thirty warriors, and women besides. But Freydis immediately violated this and took five men more, concealing them so that the brothers were not aware of this until they reached Vinland.

And so they put to sea, having a previous understanding that they would sail in consort, if circumstances permitted, and they kept near each other on the voyage, but the brothers arrived somewhat before, and had carried their belongings up to Leif's house. When Freydis came to land, her crew unloaded her ship and carried their possessions up to the house. Then Freydis remonstrated: "Why did you bring your luggage in here?"

"We supposed," the brothers replied, "that all the terms of our agreement would be kept."

"To me Leif loaned the buildings," she said, "not to you!"

Helgi remarked: "We brothers bear you no ill-will."

Then they carried their belongings out and constructed their shed [hall] and then built a shed on the bank of a lake farther from the sea, and trimmed up everything well around there. Meanwhile Freydis had trees cut down for her ship's cargo. Then as it drew toward winter, the brothers proposed that they engage in games and sports. This they did for some time, until the men began to maltreat each other and their meetings were broken off and the games stopped, and visiting ceased between the houses, and thus the winter dragged on for a long time.

Early one morning Freydis got up out of bed, dressed except for shoes, even though the weather was such that a heavy dew had fallen. She took her husband's cloak, threw it around her, and then walked to the brothers' house and to the door which had been left halfway open by one of the men who had gone out a little before. She pushed open the door and stood in the doorway for a time without speaking. Finnbogi lay on the far side of the house and was awake, and he asked: "What do you want here, Freydis?"

She answered: "I want you to get up and go out with me. I want to talk with you."

He did as she asked, and they went to a log which lay against the wall of the house and sat down on it.

"How do you like everything hereabouts?" she asked.

He replied: "I think well of what this land produces, but am ill-pleased with the enmity that there is between us, for I gave no cause for it."

"Just as you say," said she, "and that goes for me too. And so I have come to propose something. I desire to trade ships with you brothers, for yours is a larger ship, and I want to leave this country."

"I may do it," said he, "if that will make you happy."

Then they parted, she going home, and Finnbogi back to rest. When she climbed into bed, she awakened her husband Thorvard with her cold feet, and he asked why she was so chill and wet. She spoke with great rage: "I have been," said she, "to the brothers, to ask to purchase their ship, for I wish to buy the larger ship, and they took it so ill that they struck me and handled me roughly. But you, spineless man that you are, will not avenge my shame or your own! And this I have to learn, that I am no longer in Greenland! I shall separate from you unless you avenge this!"

At this he could endure her upbraidings no longer, and ordered the men to get up at once and take their weapons, and this they did. Then they went straightway to the house of the brothers, and inside, and seized them sleeping and tied them up tightly, and led each one out when he was bound, and as he came out, Freydis had each one put to death. Now all the men were slain, and only the women remained, whom no one would kill. Then Freydis spoke up: "Hand me an ax!" And when she had it, she went at the five women there and left them dead.

After this damnable deed they returned to their own house, and it was apparent that Freydis believed everything had worked out well. She spoke as follows to her companions: "If it be our lot to return to Greenland, I will take the life of any man who talks about what has happened. What we shall say is that they simply stayed on here when we left."

Early in the spring they loaded to its utmost capacity the ship the brothers had owned, and with all the good things they could get hold of. They sailed out on the high seas, and after a good voyage arrived in Eriksfjörd early in the summer.

Now Karlsefni was still there and had his ship ready for departure, and was waiting for a fair wind. Men say that no more richly laden ship ever left Greenland than the one he steered.

Freydis now went to her home, as it stood in the meantime unscathed. She gave very great gifts to all her companions, to help persuade them not to reveal her guilt. She now resumed her life at home. But all did not keep their pledge to remain silent about their crimes and wickedness, so that the story leaked out eventually. It came at last to the ear of Leif, her brother, and he thought it an altogether atrocious tale. He took three of the men who had been with Freydis and tortured them to confess the whole affair, and they all told the same story. "I cannot find it in me," said Leif, "to do that to my sister Freydis which she deserves, but I foretell this of her and her husband, that their offspring will thrive but little." From this it followed that no one thereafter thought them capable of anything but evil.

We can only guess what actually happened during the early-dawn visit of Freydis to the brothers' house. One suspects that the visit was not entirely a matter of business. Adultery by a woman was punishable by death. Freydis may have feared she had been seen in an indiscretion with the younger brother and wanted to kill all possible witnesses. It is not likely that her murder spree was an instance of going berserk. If she disposed of the bodies of her thirty-five victims by burying them in a mass grave, the proof of her crime may someday be discovered.

15

Evidences

If the grisly traces of Freydis' crime have not yet been uncovered, there are other more pleasant evidences of viking occupancy in Vinland. The first two were found in a small gully on the south shore of Follins Pond in 1952. The next two were discovered in 1960, and two others in April, 1964.

The first finding of a proved viking site in North America was the unearthing of a ship shoring in the Follins Pond gully. There is no way of telling whether the shoring was for Leif's ship. However, Leif's ship, loaned to his brother Thorvald, was shored at Leif's Shelters for four winters. Karlsefni's ship may have been shored there three winters and after that Freydis' ship—which may have been Leif's.

A ship is brought ashore prow first. The shoring stakes at varying distances from the line of keel bearings were set at a slight angle inward to abut against the overlapping strakes of the shored ship and hold it upright. The positions of these stakes showed that the ship for which the shoring had been made was also sharp at the stern.

The shoring was of a kind more primitive than any known from Colonial times, consisting of nine keel bearings, the first four posts planted on or supported by stones, then one post without a stone base, and then four stones, the tops of which had been slightly above the surface of the ground. This shoring had held the keel of a ship two to three inches above the ground, a ship of eighteen-foot beam and sixty-nine feet long. On the authoritative testimony of Howard I. Chapelle, a ship of those dimensions of any type known to have been in New England waters since the days of Columbus would have been decked and would have weighed from forty to seventy tons. The presence of the laboriously planted posts in the line of keel bearings shows that the ground had been dug away from under the stern half of the ship so that men could get under to repair planks near the keel. Therefore the shoring had supported the weight of the ship. Professor Donald M. Burmister of the Department of Civil Engineering and Soil Mechanics at Columbia University estimated that the keel bearings would have supported at most twenty-two and one-half tons. In all the history of sailing ships, the only type of vessel of the dimensions given which would have weighed less than twenty-two and one-half tons was a viking ship. A viking ship of such size would have weighed, without her equipment, from ten to thirteen tons.

At the time the shoring was uncovered, Carbon-14 dating was a new process, and the methods essential to proper collecting and protecting of specimens for testing were not generally understood. Dr. Maurice Robbins wrote me on De-

Evidence that a viking ship was once shored at Follins Pond is shown in this diagram. A line of posts and stones held the keel off the ground, while stakes planted in the shape of the ship propped it upright. A shed protected it from winter weather.

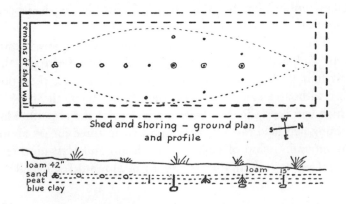

cember 4, 1959: "At the time the stakes were recovered there was no thought, at least on my part, of using them for a radio-carbon sample. In fact, during the several weeks which ensued between my taking them to the Museum and sending them to you, they were immersed in fresh water to prevent shrinking and cracking. This treatment would tend to contaminate them with fresh carbon from the water." The stakes, the largest of which was less than five inches in diameter, were never protected from fallouts from bomb testings, which invalidated all the samples (among them one from the shoring) at the Lamont Geological Laboratory. The other pieces, which were in my possession for years, were similarly unprotected.

The day before the dig by the Massachusetts Archaeological Society I had seen the remains of the inner-gully end of the ship shed, in the form of a ridge of earth eighteen inches high and twenty-three feet long, with short ridges at right angles to it in the direction of the lake. The extensive trench-digging by the M.A.S. obliterated these ridges, and through the years, until March, 1964, I supposed I was the only witness to their having existed. I am happy to be able to present two other witnesses. In rereading filed correspondence, I came across the following:

Attleboro, Mass.
Dec. 4, 1959

DEAR FRED:

Yes, I distinctly recall the earth formation which suggested some sort of shed and I also recall your mentioning this at the time.

Sincerely

MAURICE [DR. MAURICE ROBBINS]

Encouraged by finding the letter which had slipped my memory, I wrote on March 3, 1964, to Howard C. Mandell, who had been the president of the M.A.S. in 1952. He replied on March 20: "I do remember roughly rectangular ridges toward the inner end of the gully."

In 1960 the shelters of Helgi and Finnbogi were discov-

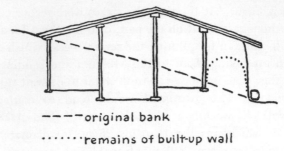

----original bank

......remains of built-up wall

In 1960, archaeologists found shelters built by Helgi and Finnbogi who, with Leif's sister, went to Vinland in search of vines, timber, and furs to sell in Europe at high prices. Because Freydis refused them accommodations in Leif's hall, the brothers were forced to build their own house, which is diagramed here in cross section.

ered. The two Icelanders, it will be remembered, "carried their belongings out and constructed their shed [*gerdu ser skala*] and then built a shed [*ok settu thann skala*] on the bank of a lake farther from the sea." They built two sheds, as Leif had done, one for themselves and their belongings, and one for their ship. Let us call them Helgi's Shelters.

The sites of Helgi's Shelters were isolated from public attention by thickets of greenbrier on the high ground and by marshy areas in which the vines are almost impassable.[1] Some weeks previous to the M.A.S. dig, I had Boy Scouts cut vines to make a clear path by which members of the M.A.S. could approach the sites without getting their clothes ripped. On November 11, 1960, seventeen members of the M.A.S. did extensive digging, and because they found no nails or other artifacts, they came to the conclusion that whatever the two sites were, they were "not Colonial." By the same token, they

[1] The story of how they were found is told in my book *Atlantic Crossings Before Columbus*, pp. 157–70. The theorizing on p. 164 about the interior layout of the house at Helgi's Shelters and the drawing of the probable plan of the house interior on p. 165 are, I now realize, in several particulars, invalid.

were not post-Colonial. Their definite rectangularity and the nature of the soil in the bank demonstrated that they were no casual sand pits left by cranberry-bog makers.

The curve of the shore line of Mill Pond a thousand years ago was such that the length of the house was almost parallel to the bank's edge, while the ship shed was end-on to the water. The sheds were 130 feet apart. The ship shed was close to twenty feet wide with visible remains fifty-three and one-half feet in length.

The interior length of the house at Helgi's Shelters was forty-three feet four inches, and the interior width was eighteen feet. It contained two sleeping platforms, each at least six feet broad. These were perhaps a foot or more in height, consisting of earth not so deeply excavated as the central corridor. The earth at the edges of the platform was no doubt retained by two or more horizontal logs about six inches in diameter, one lying above the other and held in position by abutment against the vertical roof-supporting posts. The positioning of several stones and some soil discoloration gave evidence that there had been what one of the M.A.S. diggers called "some sort of construction" near the hard-pan floor along what would have been the edges of the sleeping platforms. A concentration of stones extended across the interior of the house about seven feet from the door end. These stones seem to be evidence that there was an interior wall, now collapsed, which retained the ends of the sleeping platforms and also partitioned off the east end of the house to provide space for stacking bulky implements and utensils.

To keep the weight of the roof off the edges of the undisturbed bank and especially off the built-up wall of earth and sod, there had to be vertical posts along the inner sides of each wall. It was customary to have a row of roof-supporting posts along the edge of each sleeping platform, forming three aisles in the hall. Each pole was firmly planted on a stone at the bottom of a shallow hole, with the earth tamped in around it. The house at Helgi's Shelters must have had about thirty roof-supporting posts. The roof consisted of small timbers twelve feet long, laid rather close to each other and extending from the ridge pole toward either side. Brush laid over these supported a two- or two-and-a-half-inch layer of sod, grass side down, and over that was a layer of thatch or bent, probably meadow grass, for waterproofing. The weight of the sod would keep the roof from being blown away in a storm, and the sod was an excellent conserver of heat.

The *Flateyjarbok* tells us that Freydis, standing in the open doorway, was seen by Finnbogi, who lay on the far side of the house (*la innastr i skalanum*; literally, "lay inmost in the hall"). The letter *F* in the diagram marks the approximate position where Finnbogi lay. But if Freydis stood in the doorway through the stone partition, then Finnbogi occupied the single sleeping platform at the opposite end of the hall.

With the partitioning stone wall, the interior length of the house at Mill Pond takes on special significance. The standard width of sleeping space for persons lying beside each other is twenty-seven inches, half the width of a standard double bed. In the house at Helgi's Shelters there was a width

Early one morning when Helgi and Finnbogi were still asleep, Freydis persuaded her husband to kill them and all their crew. Then she loaded with goods the ship they had owned and sailed home to Greenland. This is the floor plan of the brothers' house. The "F" in the diagram indicates where Finnbogi was sleeping.

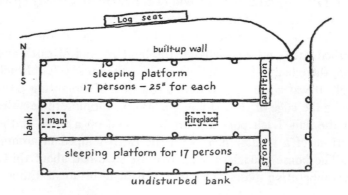

of sleeping space of twenty-five inches for each of the thirty men and five women. The house was precisely of the minimum length required for a party of thirty-five persons. The interior length becomes a corroborating point in the identification of Helgi's Shelters.

In viking dwellings the hearth was customarily sunk a little below the floor level, and generally was lined with flagstones. In house sites we often find the largest tree growing above a hearth, since carbon facilitates the breakdown of soil and the formation of bacteria which provide plant food. The largest tree at Helgi's Shelters stands near the middle of the hollow, on the longitudinal median line and "about five feet nearer to the door end than the west end." [2]

To dig for possible datable charcoal under the tree in Helgi's house site, it would be necessary to procure the permission of the owner of the land to cut down the tree. Until that permission is obtained, and while the tree stands, the hearth in Helgi's house remains untouched, awaiting professional archaeological investigation.

Paul N. Jago of North Quincy, Massachusetts, has made a survey of the entire area of Helgi's Shelters with accurate measurements of distances and directions, and his graph-paper map has been of great assistance. The best trail in to the Helgi ship-shed site starts from behind the Hickman house, which is to the southeast from the Helgi sheds. A direct route to Helgi's Shelters is indicated in the illustration by the broken line marked "trail." There is a third trail starting from behind the Rodney Hall house, which is to the southwest of the Helgi sheds. This takes one to near the shore of Mill Pond, whence one must work his way to the east through briers. In 1964, we found the first two of these trails effectively

---

[2] In advance of the M.A.S. dig, I went to the office of the assessors, Town of Yarmouth, at South Yarmouth, to get the name of the owner of the land where we wished to dig. They told me it was Mrs. Frederick Hickman, and I obtained her written permission. At the end of the dig we learned that the house site was on an adjoining property. I feel responsible for an unintentional and most regrettable blunder, and I hope the owner, Rodney E. Hall, has forgiven it.

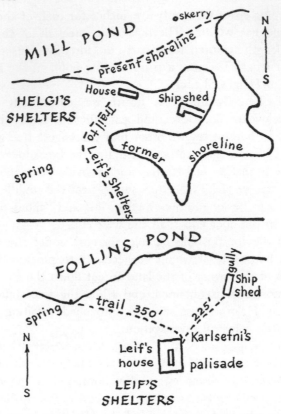

In this diagram is the site where Leif Erikson probably built his hall, around which Thorfinn Karlsefni later put up a strong, high fence. Part of the trail to the spring is still visible, as is part of the trail from Helgi's Shelters to Leif's Shelters.

blocked by briers, so that entrance without a machete had become impossible.

In addition to the ship shed and the shoring at Follins Pond, and the two sheds at Mill Pond, other evidences of viking occupancy of the area were discovered in 1964. When I first went to Follins Pond in 1947, I was looking for runic inscriptions on rocks, and mooring holes in rocks, and rock foundations of Leif's house. I had rocks on the brain. On the top of what seemed to be the highest hill along the south shore of Follins Pond, I saw a hollow as large across as a sizable cellar hole, but it was shallow. Because it had no cellar walls, I assumed it was a natural sink. For seventeen years I remembered it, but was not plagued by it, as I should have been. During those years I acquired experience in excavating the sites of half-cellar, earth-wall houses of Acadian French in Nova Scotia. In these houses no stones had been used except in the fireplace and chimney and as bases for posts to support the roof. The remains of the walls at the end of the ship shed at Follins Pond had no visible foundation stones. The house at Mill Pond, except for the partition wall, had been of sod.

In 1964, Father Michael Wolfe, who has done considerable archaeological work at Brattahlid, wrote me: "What we are beginning to realize more fully is that the *landnam* Norsemen [early settlers] built extensively in sod, and the more obvious stone ruins which dot the terrain are most likely from later periods."

In 1958, my friend William L. Smyth had loaned me aerial photographs taken in 1947, when the whole area near the Follins Pond gully was in pristine condition, except for one house occupied by Mr. and Mrs. S. A. Canty. However, before I had seen the photographs, I had visited the area and found that the entire south shore of Follins Pond had been bulldozed for a housing development advertised as "the place the Norsemen called Paradise when they landed here in the eleventh century." Two photographs of the area showed some large circles or curved lines which on-the-ground investigation proved to be natural contour lines. At the same time the photographs showed an oval with a dark center like an eye. This was on the brow of the hill above and slightly to the east of the gully, at what seemed a possible site for Leif's house. I assumed that the dark spot might have been Leif's house site, and the oval Karlsefni's palisade. I had no way to prove this, for a large house and automobile turnaround now cover it. Actually the oval was not large enough to have been the remains of Karlsefni's "strong fence of palings." Although a palisade around two rows of houses with plenty of space might well take an oval shape, it is unlikely that a palisade would have been an oval that just cleared the corners of a house it was designed to protect. A circle or an oval seen in an aerial photograph may be the natural contour of a hill, but a perfect rectangle is not natural and can be only the work of man.

When my editor Martin Mann asked me to "recheck all evidences," I again borrowed the aerial photographs. I again saw the small oval in the photographs. This time I was overwhelmed by what I saw: a dark spot in the middle of a large and perfect rectangle! There could be no doubt that this rectangle was man-made. Here seemed to be positive evidence of a palisade of the sort the saga says Karlsefni erected around Leif Erikson's house in Vinland. Had the actual site of Leif's house and Karlsefni's palisade been located at last?

The elongated dark spot in the center of the rectangle was at the highest point of the highest hill anywhere near the gully. The door of the house would have been on a long side of the house near one end. Logically it would have been on the east side near the northeast corner, from which the occupants could most quickly descend to the gully to defend their shored ship. The gateway in the palisade would have been on the east side opposite the door.

The northeast corner of the rectangle was only 200 feet from the inner end of the Follins Pond gully, and only 100 yards from the most active spring in the neighborhood. This is the spring in the bank below and slightly to the west of the Canty house, with a flow of six quarts a minute, over 2,000 gallons a day. The presence of that copious spring must have been one of the principal factors in Leif's decision to build a house for the winter nearby. Undoubtedly the view and the nearness to where he saw he could shore his ship also played an important part in his choice.

Down the slope of the palisade hill toward the spring, in a line that would cut directly through the wall of the Canty house, there is a trail whose hard-packed surface, two inches below the flanking surface of the ground, has in patches prevented the growth of vegetation upon it. This trail stops abruptly at the retaining wall of the Canty garden and obviously existed before the building of the Canty house. After the ship had been shored, there would have been little occasion for Leif's, Thorvald's, or Karlsefni's men to go down to the gully except perhaps to relieve a guard there. But whenever one of the men was thirsty, he would run down to the spring to drink, and thus at least thirty men during each of eight winters trod the trail to the spring several times a day. It was unlikely that water was carried up the hill in buckets except for cooking purposes and for emergency fire fighting.

On level ground twenty-eight feet from the edge of the bank above the spring there is a fireplace, apparently circular, with large stones. This invites investigation by a professional archaeologist.

In the middle of the rectangle, the size of the dark spot showing the shadowed house-site hollow cannot be determined with accuracy from the photographs. However, we do know the size (forty-eight by fifteen feet) of the interior of Erik's one-room house at Brattahlid, which had only one sleeping platform, and of the house at Mill Pond, which had two. Leif's house in Vinland must have been larger than his father's Greenland hall. There are three reasons for this statement. First, Leif was building a house that would have sleeping space for his thirty-five men and himself, and therefore it was as long as his father's hall. Second, he could easily make it wider because he had at hand plenty of timber for posts to support the roof and to construct roof beams. Third, the eighteen-foot width of the house at Helgi's Shelters and the seventeen- to eighteen-foot interior width of the original house at Narssaq farm in Greenland argue for a like width of Leif's house.

We cannot be far wrong if we assume that Leif's house

was eighteen feet wide (wide enough for two sleeping platforms) and at least forty-five feet long on the inside. With the earth excavated to a depth of about two and one-half feet, he had enough material to build walls to a height of four feet above ground. He thus had six and one-half feet of clearance between floor and roof, enough for him to stand upright, if the six-foot-two-inch skeleton unearthed in the graveyard of the church at Brattahlid was, as some think, his. The walls were tamped down, with sod outside to prevent rain erosion. The roof of course overhung the walls. The walls must have been at least four feet thick. There were no windows. The only openings were a door and a hole in the roof above the fireplace.

The exterior size of the house was something like 53 or more feet long and about 26 feet wide. In the aerial photographs the large rectangle seems to be a little over 110 feet long and about 92 feet wide. These dimensions suggest that Karlsefni laid out the palisade with the Norse fathmur measure: 18 fathmurs (111 feet) long, and 15 fathmurs (92½ feet) wide. The space between the outside walls of the house and the palisade was at least 29 feet at the ends and over 30 feet on the long sides. This was about right for convenience and safety. All trees nearby outside the palisade were of course cut down so that no enemy could climb up to see over the palisade. One tall tree inside the palisade would have been left standing to furnish a post to watch for Skraelings coming out of the forest.

I arranged for a private dig in September, 1964, under the direction of Mrs. Robert D. Barnes.[3] The other members of the party included her husband, who also had had much archaeological experience, F. Newton Miller of the Metropolitan Chapter of the New York Archaeological Association, who had dug for post molds with Dr. William A. Ritchie, New York State archaeologist. For the record, Mr. and Mrs. Barnes established by compass a grid on North-South, East-

[3] Mrs. Barnes was trained by Glenn A. Black at Angel Mounds in the search for post molds.

West lines, based on the cement boundary marker on the northern brow of the hill west of the road. The rectangle itself is slightly off North-South alignment.

Three five-foot squares were dug near the brow of the hill on the east side. These established that beneath about two inches of friable turf there were about three inches of loam-sand mixture. Below that, down to a depth of three feet, there was yellow sand of consistent color. With the exception of a few spots of charcoal, indicating that there had been a forest fire in the area, the three squares were sterile. It began to look as though our search might be very protracted and disappointing. But Newton Miller cheered us with the observation that in such light-colored sand any existing post molds would be clearly visible and unmistakable. The place where any man-planted post had rotted away would appear as a discoloration decidedly darker than that sand.

Repeated measurements on the early aerial photographs and on photographs subsequent to the bulldozing, road building, and housing development indicated the position of the rectangle in relation to the road which now crossed it. They showed that the east side of the rectangle was at least fifteen feet from the three squares. Would digging across the line of the side of the rectangle reveal post molds? With faith that it would (and I say faith because there was no surface indication of what the aerial photographs revealed), I dug a narrow trench across the line. I found nothing; but later, on September 19, I enlarged that trench to a properly orientated five-foot square, and post molds appeared! Immediately the other persons present dug squares adjacent to mine, and still others adjacent to those. In all the squares dug for more than thirty-five feet there appeared a North-South pattern of post molds extending in a line.

The average depth of the molds was nine to ten inches, and their diameters were from three to five inches. Some of them narrowed near the bottom and ended in a point, showing that they had been sharpened posts thrust into the sand. The post molds did not touch each other, nor were they in precise alignment, but were in zigzag formation. The palisade wall had been a wattle fence of spaced posts, with interwoven branches no doubt tied in with interlacing thorny vines. Every ten feet or so there seems to have been a post of larger diameter, or the trunk of a large tree which was incorporated into the fence to give it complete stability. Karlsefni's strong fence of palings was erected with a minimum of effort and without any ridging of earth as an embankment on the inside of the fence. This is why there is nothing visible on the ground to indicate the sides of the rectangle. It seemed marvelous that aerial photographs (scale: 1 inch = 1,200 feet) could reveal what on-the-ground beholders could not see! After we had established the precise position of the palisade, we observed that its sides followed the ground as it begins to fall off from the top level of the hill.

Complete investigation of the whole area of the palisade hill calls for a professional archaeologist, with a grant from a foundation, and permission from the owners, who have placed in my hands the assigning of that permission. More than 300 feet of the sides of the palisade remain untouched by the bulldozers, and we have dug only 10 per cent of them. Most of the house hollow seems to have been removed by the bulldozing across the hill, but it seems likely that careful investigation will uncover some of the east edge of the house site. A thorough investigation, besides establishing the precise size of the palisade, should find artifacts, a kitchen midden, and pits of datable charcoal.

While we look forward to more extensive archaeological investigation, it is not premature to state that the site satisfies in all respects the geographical description of Leif's camp in Vinland as recorded in the sagas. Moreover, the two shed sites in the bank of Mill Pond and the ship shed and shoring in the Follins Pond gully are in the exact relationship to one another that was noted in the saga.

In the "infinite variety of nature," in the infinite universe, there are probably many planets where all eighteen geographical requirements (see Appendix I) in the Vinland sagas can be met. We are, however, not dealing with the infinite, but with this finite earth, and on this planet there is only one area, the south shore of Follins Pond and the south shore of Mill Pond, where all these requirements are satisfied; and, in addition, we have in that area the six archaeological facts to clinch the demonstration.

16

Ebbing Tide

There is a record of only one more voyage to Vinland in viking times: "1047. Trond Halfdanson flies from Norway, and after visiting Vinland, on his return to Greenland is driven up on the coast there and dies of exposure. His body is taken back to Norway." An important man, his name was kept in the records, but without any detailed account of where he had been.

The viking period ended about 1075, but we shall here trace briefly what happened to Greenland down to the time of Columbus.

As a result of Karlsefni's decision to relinquish the attempt to colonize Vinland, the Greenlanders accepted the impracticality of such an enterprise. After Karlsefni finally sailed home from Greenland about 1015, knowledge of Vinland began to fade. Confusions crept in, and we read in the manuscript, in the Arnamagnaean Library (A.M. 107) such an uncertainty as this: "Southward from Greenland is Helluland; then is Markland; then it is not far to Wineland the Good, which some men believe extends from Africa, and if this be so, then there is an open sea flowing in between Wineland and Markland." The Greenland vikings went only as far as Markland for timber. There is one record in the Icelandic Annals: "1327. A ship arrives in Iceland from Greenland, with 17 men. It had been to Markland."

The increasing uncertainty as to what coasts Karlsefni and his predecessors had explored carried over into confusions as to "Whitemen's Land," which is called by some persons

"Ireland the Great." The question here is not whether the Irish preceded the vikings in reaching North America. It would not be surprising if the Irish did, and some believe that references in Norse literature testify to that effect, though careful scrutiny of those references leaves the point in doubt. Undeniably, however, it was through vikings who traded in Ireland that we have a record of Irishmen and Icelanders who together visited Ireland the Great, and there saw Ari Marson held by the natives as their chief. From other vikings who traded in Ireland we have a far more circumstantial story of how the natives in Ireland the Great had a viking named Bjorn Asbrandson as their chief and would not let him depart. The Asbrandson story is in Appendix II. The Ari Marson reference we shall here consider.

Rafn, an Icelander, who traded much in Ireland and was in consequence called the Limerick Merchant, told of a relative of his, Ari Marson, who was found living in Whitemen's Land. It seems that the natives there, wherever it was, had recognized Ari's superior abilities and would not let him leave them. The details that Rafn put into the story are that south from inhabited Greenland there are deserts, uninhabited places, and icebergs, then the Skraelings, then Markland, then Vineland the Good; next, and somewhat behind lies Whitemen's Land; there Irishmen and Icelanders recognized Ari the son of Mar and Katla of Reykjanes, of whom nothing had been heard for a long time, and who had been made a chief there by the inhabitants.

To what land did this "somewhat behind Vineland" point? Some think it meant in the interior, back from the Vinland seacoast, and believing this, they confuse Ireland the Great with presumable Bronze-Age occupancy of the megalithic structures at North Salem, New Hampshire, and elsewhere in the interior of New England. Some think "behind Vineland" meant farther south along the seacoast than Karlsefni had explored—in the Carolinas or Florida.

The *Landnamabok* gives a definite and much more persuasive location for Ireland the Great:

Ari Marson was drifted on the ocean to Whitemen's Land, which some persons call Ireland the Great. It lies westward in the ocean near Vineland the good; to it men say that there is six days' sailing from Ireland due west. Ari could not depart thence, and was baptized there.

The phrases "in the ocean" and "near Vineland" and "six days' sailing from Ireland due west" seem to leave no room for doubt as to what land meets the geographical requirements of Ari Thorgilsson's description of Ireland the Great. It must have been the great island only eleven miles off the coast of Vinland, the island which Leif Erikson named Helluland, and Karlsefni called Biarney. We find much to support this identification. Newfoundland is the only large island that fits the description; it is one more than six, actually seven days' sailing distance out of sight of land west of Ireland. The northern end of Newfoundland is at the latitude of the southern end of Ireland. (This, however, is not to suggest that the settlement at L'Anse-aux-Meadow in northern Newfoundland was not viking but Irish.)

The notion of a distant country of the dead, a Whitemen's Land which was an Ireland the Great to the west, was known in Celtic tradition and in the folklore of various seaside people in Europe. Karlsefni too had this notion. The earliest reference to it in the viking voyages was in *Hauksbok*, in what was said by the two boys Karlsefni kidnapped from their parents in Markland:

"They said there lay a land over against their land, the inhabitants of which wore white clothes and carried poles before them festooned with rags [religious banners] and yelled loudly [chanted]. People believe this must have been White Man's Land or Great Ireland." The obvious description of a religious procession, the white garments of a missionary order, banners and chanting, is too circumstantial for the Indian boys to have invented. From evidence (for which see Appendix IV), we know that in the fourteenth century the Indians of Nova Scotia knew of the existence of Newfoundland. Moreover, there was some communication and trade between Nova

Scotia and Newfoundland, and perhaps since the inhabitants of Newfoundland in the fourteenth century had "Latin books, which they at the present time do not understand," missionaries had been there.

During the first hundred years after Leif Erikson, Christianity spread until it dominated Greenland. Eventually, twelve parish churches were built in the settlements, with two monastic houses and St. Michael's Convent of Benedictine nuns. There were four churches on the east coast, and in a later century, the Dominican Monastery of St. Thomas also.

Bishop Eric Gnupson, a Norwegian, arrived in Greenland in 1112. The first bishop of Greenland and Vinland, geographically the largest diocese in all Christendom, he chose for his see a site near the head of Einarsfjörd, the fjord immediately to the south of Eriksfjörd. There at Gardar, at a location accessible from Eriksfjörd by a short walk, he had his episcopal farm. At Gardar was erected a cathedral 80 feet long by 45 feet wide, and a bishop's palace with a great hall 50 feet by 24 feet. A conscientious and enterprising man, Bishop Gnupson set sail in 1121 to visit Vinland, the other portion of his diocese, but did not return. He was believed to have perished, and after two years, Socke Thorarsson, a descendant of Erik the Red, sent a request to the jurisdictional ecclesiastical authorities in Europe for a new and permanent bishop.

More than a century later Pope Gregory IX received an unprecedented request relating to Greenland sent him by the archbishop of Trondhjem who by then had supervision over the bishopric of Gardar. This was the pope's reply in May, 1237:

You state, beloved brother, that in some churches of your suffragans it is impossible to have the Eucharist, because of the scarcity of wheat and that wine can never or hardly be had in those countries, and you ask whether it is allowed to deceive the people with some simulation of piety and to distribute to them mere oblations made of some other substance, and give them beer or some other beverage instead of wine. To this we answer that by no means can you do either of those

*things, because bread of wheat and wine of grapes, conse-
crated through the ministry of the priest by the words of the
Creator must needs be the elements of the Sacraments.*

Officials residing in comfort in Europe simply could not
imagine the conditions of living in a land where wheat could
not grow and where the importation of wheat and wine or
anything could be accomplished only by exertions pushed to
the limit of human endurance with extreme peril across hundreds of miles of stormy ocean. With the Church a tool of the
State, Greenland got into the political basket, and in 1246 the
see of Trondhjem sent out Bishop Olaf to persuade Greenlanders to submit to the Norwegian crown. He argued with
success, and fifteen years later Greenland surrendered the
independence which Erik the Red had achieved.

Nevertheless, exploration continued. In about 1266 a voyage was made to the Arctic under the auspices of the Greenland bishopric, and four years thereafter a clergyman brought
home to Norway a description of Eskimos.

In 1285 Icelanders—not Greenlanders—found land "to
the westward off Iceland." This was supposedly a fresh discovery, but note the uncertainty as to whether it was land never
before known. Five years later, three men who may have been
Greenlanders, but were more likely Icelanders, sailed for 1,000
miles up the west coast of Greenland to 72° 57' North. They
wintered on an island now called Kingiktorsuak. The next
spring, long before the pack ice permitted them to return
south, they left a record of their presence there in the Arctic
in the form of a runic inscription on a small stone in a cairn,
giving their names and the date: "Erling Sigvatsson and
Bjarni Thordarson and Endridi Oddsson raised these beacons
April 25, 1291."

The population of Greenland, though it taxed to the limit
the country's resources, was at most somewhat under 3,000. A
record of 1327 shows that 6,912 Peter's pence were sent from
Greenland to Rome. That sum had probably been due for
about three years.

In the early 1340's Eskimos invaded the Western Settlement. When the unhappy news reached the Eastern Settlement, Ivar Bardson, the episcopal administrator, visited the invaded fjords and wrote a report which was delivered to Norway. "The land was laid waste, churches were destroyed. Only 9 parishes escaped. The people of both sexes were carried away as prisoners. Many of them returned."

The encroachments of the Eskimos hampered the Greenlanders, whose best hunting ground for walrus and narwhal was in the Disco Bay area at 70° North. The product of Greenland most prized in Europe was ivory, but hurtful competition came from Norwegians who hunted walrus and narwhal near Novaya Zemlya. Then Europe began importing African elephant tusks. Norway instituted a shortsighted policy of monopoly of trade with Greenland limited to Bergen merchants. Finally in the mid-fourteenth century the Black Death so reduced the population of Norway that the country itself fell victim to merchant invaders. One trading ship, sent out once a year from Bergen, kept the Greenland settlements alive. The merchants of the Hanseatic League put a stop to this limited contact. There was still some trade between Greenland and other countries, as evidenced by what is believed to be a fourteenth-century building called the "Greenland Fishery" in King's Lynn in England, and the extraordinary record that in the year 1380 "four ships at the same time reached Greenland." Greenlanders were pinched by lessening supplies, and by about 1410 were practically forgotten.

Although appointments to the bishopric of Gardar were continued, they became merely nominal. In the first 150 years, beginning with Bishop Gnupson, there had been nine bishops appointed, seven of whom reached Gardar. In the 250 years thereafter, seventeen bishops of Greenland were consecrated, but most of them never resided at Gardar or were even required to go there.[1] In 1448 Pope Nicholas V wrote that there had been no priests in Greenland for thirty years, and in

[1] *Diplomatarium Norvegicum*, Vol. 17B, lists thirty bishops of Greenland with their dates from 1112 to 1537.

1490 Pope Alexander VI wrote to Matthias Knutsson, soon thereafter appointed to the Gardar bishopric: "We are informed that on account of the freezing of the sea, no ship has touched Greenland and no resident Bishop or priest has reached its church for the last 80 years."

The disappearance of some Greenland farms, according to the archaeologist Aage Roussel, was due to three causes: landslides, changes of river beds, and submergence of the coast, "which has amounted to 5 or 6 meters since the time of the settlements." The deterioration of the population of Greenland resulted from insufficiencies of diet and intermarriage with Eskimos. The burials in permafrost show progressive teeth decay and dwindling stature.

While Leif Erikson lived, the Greenlanders felt they were part of a growing, thriving community. With his death hopes died. Gradually they lost all traces of their viking past. A great chapter in the history of people from Scandinavian origin drew to its close.

I

The Location of Vinland

Fifty writers have propounded about thirty theories as to the location of Leif Erickson's Vinland campsite:

Location	Proponents
Greenland	Hugh Murray, 1829; A. J. Weise, 1884
Labrador	T. W. Higginson, 1882; L. G. Power, 1887; M. L. Fernald, 1915
St. Lawrence Valley	H. P. Steensby, 1917; Andrew Fossum, 1918
Ontario-Great Lakes	J. W. Curran, 1939; Corrado Gini, 1960
Newfoundland	William Robertson, 1777; J. R. Forster, 1784; W. A. Munn, 1914; A. H. Mallery, 1951; H. Ingstad, 1963
New Brunswick	M. F. Howley, 1898
Nova Scotia	Gustav Storm, 1889; Juul Diserud, 1901; Joseph Fischer, 1903
New England	A. M. Reeves, 1906; J. E. Olson, 1913; Matthias Thórdarson, 1930; Halldór Hermannsson, 1936
Maine	Edward Reman, 1949
New Hampshire	W. B. Goodwin, 1941
Boston, latitude of	Henry Wheaton, 1831; E. N. Horsford, 1892
Kingston Bay	Charles Boland, 1961
Cape Cod	Abner Morse, 1861; A S. Packard, 1888; William Hovgaard, 1914;

Location	*Proponents*
	G. M. Gathorne-Hardy, 1921; C. H. L. Jones and T. H. Raddall, 1934; A. W. Brögger, 1937; H. R. Holand, 1946; F. J. Pohl, 1948; J. Kr. Tornöe, 1964
Martha's Vineyard	E. F. Gray, 1930
Rhode Island	C. C. Rafn, 1837; N. L. Beamish, 1841; J. G. Kohl, 1869; B. F. De-Costa, 1889
New York	J. W. Moulton and J. V. N. Yates, 1824
Rhode Island to New Jersey	Paul Gaffarel, 1869
Pennsylvania or Virginia	G. A. Westman, 1757
Cape Cod to Virginia	W. H. Babcock, 1913; E. I. Haugen, 1942
Pennsylvania to Carolina	P. F. Suhm, 1760
Carolina	M. C. Sprengel, 1782
Georgia-Florida	O. S. Reuter, 1934
Coast of the U.S.A.	Luka Jelíc, 1894

Even if no evidence of viking habitation had been found in the Follins Pond area of Cape Cod, the geographical clues supplied by the sagas are sufficient to locate Leif's campsite. At any rate, the Greenlanders found the site on the basis of the first twelve of the following eighteen clues:

1. The farthest land to which Leif sailed was southwest from Greenland.

2. The land was five days' sailing distance southwest of Bjarni's third land.

3. An island lay north of the land.

4. From that island Leif sailed with the wind of "a fair day" into a "sound." After clearing from a northeaster, in the northern hemisphere the wind shifts in a clockwise direction, blowing first from the southeast, then from the south, and fi-

nally from the southwest. It follows that Leif sailed north and west into the sound.

5. Leif came to the mouth of a river while the tide was ebbing. His ship was stranded in shallow water there for four or five hours.

6. From the river mouth it was "a long distance to look to the sea." In viking terms, seen from mast height, the ocean, or a line of dunes which marked where the ocean was, was close to the limit of horizon visibility.

7. From the sound Leif and his men took the ship up the river to a lake.

8. From the activities of Leif and his men, the first day we know they had at least four hours of sailing from the island to the mouth of the river, or sixteen to twenty miles, which was the distance between the two.

9. From the astronomical observations of the sun's azimuth, we know that Leif's camp was at a latitude between 41° and 42° North.

10. It was in a region where the grass withered slightly in winter, and Leif observed that it looked as though there would be plenty of fodder for cattle all winter.

11. Vines grew there as well as timber.

12. "Wineberries" grew there.

To these clues other vikings subsequently added six more:

13. To the west of Leif's camp lay vast inland waters that required a whole summer to explore.

14. Leif's camp was on a sandy cape. To the east of the camp the cape extended toward the north. Thorvald sailed eastward from Leif's campsite to the outside of a sandy cape and then northward.

15. The general line of seacoast from Leif's camp was to the west on one side of the cape and to the north on the other side. Farther on in this direction the coast led "to the east" to a fjord that had several mouths.

16. Linked to Leif's lake by a waterway wide and deep enough for a viking ship was another lake "farther from the sea"; that is, to the west of Leif's lake.

17. Somewhere beyond Leif's camp, farther from Greenland, was a north shore on whose eastern portion there were long sands. Beginning at some point along that shore, and from there to the west, were many bays.

18. A long distance to the north from Leif's camp was a place where a river flowed down from east to west.

II

A Viking Settlement in Northern Newfoundland

In Leif Erikson's time a viking settlement existed at the northern tip of Newfoundland. A Norwegian archaeologist, Anne Stine Ingstad, has unearthed the foundations of nine buildings and a primitive smithy near the present fishing village of L'Anse-aux-Meadow.[1] The positions of the turf or sod walls were revealed by slight ridges. The largest house in this settlement measured about 55 feet by 70 feet; it contained five rooms and a great hall with a central fireplace. The smithy stood nearby. Mrs. Ingstad found a stone anvil, and near it slag and small pieces of processed iron. She also uncovered the charcoal site where bog iron had been smelted for tools and weapons. Several rusty nails, a stone bowl, and a scrap of worked bronze were also uncovered.

The structures and ember pits seemed to be almost identical in type with those of some known viking farmsteads. The archaeologists from five nations who have inspected the site all agree the settlement was viking. If further proof were needed, a piece of carved soapstone, one and one-quarter inches wide, flat at the bottom and rounded on top, was dis-

[1] Anse is a French word meaning "a little deep bay." The original form of the full name on old maps was "L'Anse-aux-Medée," meaning "Little Bay of Medea," and Medea, it may be remembered, was a cruel enchantress who strewed the sea with the limbs of her brother. The name has been incorrectly anglicized, for it has no connection whatsoever with meadow.

covered in August, 1964, by Tony Beardsley. The soapstone was part of a flywheel or whorl of a wool-spinning spindle. A definite viking artifact, it was found outside on the sunny side of a house site.

The settlement lay on a windswept beach terrace about twelve feet above the sea. There was no sheltering forest and no timber except driftwood. The nearest trees were nine miles away, and they were stunted evergreens too small for shipbuilding. The soil on the northern tip of Newfoundland was largely scoured away by the ice sheet in glacial times. Only a thin layer has developed since—too poor to support crops. Vegetation could be but feeble and was greatly hindered by high winds. This is, in fact, a bleak and forbidding region of fog and deep snows; Newfoundlanders say it has only two seasons—August and winter. The settlement could not and did not last long. Radiocarbon datings of thirteen samples of charcoal indicate the settlement was occupied for a brief period near the end of the tenth century. The dates cluster around the year A.D. 1000, which was the end rather than the beginning of occupancy.

Dr. Helge Ingstad, Mrs. Ingstad's husband, has asserted that the viking settlement could have been Leif Erikson's Vinland camp. However, the L'Anse-aux-Meadow settlement does not by any stretch of the imagination fit the description in the sagas. It satisfies fewer than six of the eighteen geographical requirements. It is not up a river at the shore of a lake. There are no vines in Newfoundland. And so on.

The settlement is actually significant because, as Dr. Junius B. Bird, curator of archaeology at the American Museum of Natural History in New York, and Dr. Henry B. Collins, an anthropologist at the Smithsonian Institution have both pointed out, it constitutes "incontrovertible proof" that the vikings crossed the entire width of the North Atlantic to North America. To people in the United States, Newfoundland appears on a map far off the coast of North America. But the distance across the narrowest portion of the Strait of Belle Isle is only eleven (some say nine) miles. From the European point of view, Newfoundland is an offshore island that essentially belongs to the continent of North America. It is closer to that continent than the British Isles to continental Europe. Though many persons seem to have a mental drag, like a sea anchor, against accepting long pre-Columbian voyages out of sight of land, it is obvious that the vikings having reached Newfoundland could have reached the continent. Moreover, it would be incredible if they had failed to do so. For even the most skeptical, L'Anse-aux-Meadow casts a new light on the many evidences of the vikings that have been found on our continent.

The saga tells us that twenty-five ships loaded with men, women, children, and domestic animals set sail from Iceland with Erik in the year 986, and that only fourteen of these reached Greenland. Some of the other eleven ships got back to Iceland, but some disappeared. It is most likely that one of those loaded ships, driven south by the Labrador Current, got ashore on the northern end of Newfoundland. The viking settlement there fits perfectly into the frame of the saga.

There was no saga record of the L'Anse-aux-Meadow settlement for the simple reason that none of the vikings who were there returned to tell about it. To my mind the most significant fact is that no evidence of any ship shed close to and end-on to water has been found at or near the settlement. The ship that brought the settlers was wrecked on or before the landing. There are only nine house sites, suggesting that the population was small. The survivors eventually may have built boats of driftwood covered with hides in an attempt to row away. They may have been lost at sea. On the other hand they may have been captured by Indians. If so, this would explain the unusual physical characteristics of Indians of the Beothuk tribe of Newfoundland. The Beothuks were called Red Indians, but the color was not natural; they painted themselves with red ocher. The Miller map of 1520 says: "Corte Real brought from this region men of the same color as ourselves." Hakluyt says: "They are very white. If they were apparelled as the French are, they would be as white and as fair." Pietro Andrea Mattioli's map of Terra Nova in the Ptolemy edition of 1547–48 says: "It is a fair race." John Guy's *Narrative* (1612) is more specific: "The color of their hair was divers, some blacke, some browne, and some yellow." Beothuk hair had a softness unlike that of North American Indians. Among them were men of considerable stature, in this respect different from most if not all the aborigines of North America. Many were over six feet, some over seven feet tall. A skeleton in the museum in St. John's, Newfoundland, measures six feet four inches. The skin and hair color and the stature of the Beothuks may well have resulted from intermarriage with the vikings.

Early records seem to indicate that in battle Beothuks fought to the death. This was in the viking tradition. Later, as pilferers of white men's nets and traps, they were ruthlessly shot down at sight by the colonists, and the few remnants of the tribe fled and hid until they were exterminated. Their birchbark canoes were "in the form of a new moone, stem and stern alike" (John Guy's *Narrative*). John Gardner, in five articles in *National Fisherman*, February to June 1965, shows that their canoes, averaging fourteen feet to twenty-two feet in length, and possessing keels, in shape and construction resembled Norse types of boats unchanged since viking times. Their canoes weighed on the average one hundred pounds, and carried four to seven persons. The Beothuks propelled them by paddles, and also by oars ten feet long and made of two pieces of wood fitted together. They occasionally used a sail. They had a tradition of the sword, a weapon no other Amerindians used: "In this country there is no iron, but they make swords of a kind of stone. . . . There has been brought home a piece of a broken sword, inlaid with gold, which we can pronounce undoubtedly to have been made in Italy." (Pietro Pasqualigo in *Paese novamente retrovati*, 1501.) Beothuk winter storehouses had gable-ended roofs with carpentry equal to that of white settlers. They had drinking cups of soapstone. Their garment was a one-piece "cassock" of caribou skin, and we know that those worn by the women were hooded. Perhaps those worn by the men were also. The Beothuks seem to have had the pre-Christian viking belief in Valhalla: "They believed that the dead went into a far country to make merry with their friends." (Anspach's *History of Newfoundland*, 1818.) They had the Norsemen's respect for women. The last surviving group of Beothuks was seen in 1824. The last individual, a woman, died in 1829.

However, the 480 words of their vocabulary that have been recorded show no intrusion of the Norse language. Consider what might have happened. A few tall viking men from a small settlement like that at L'Anse-aux-Meadow, captured by the aborigines, would have been physically much admired by the Indian squaws. There would have been much interbreeding. The viking individuals would have been separated from each other and scattered among the Indians, so that no one of them could teach his own language to his children; and in time he would almost forget his own speech. Those of his offspring who had the tall stature would be more successful in hunting and would tend to survive in battle. Perhaps they resisted better the diseases introduced by Europeans after Columbus. By natural selection through the centuries the viking physical type would become proportionately more numerous. There could have been widespread racial admixture without linguistic trace.

Pertinent to what has been said about the Beothuks of Newfoundland is the story of Ari Marson of Reykjanes in Iceland, driven by storms in 983 to "Great Ireland" and there baptized. He was there "held in great respect" by the natives who would not let him depart. Rasmus B. Anderson in his Preface to the new edition (1883) of *America Not Discovered by Columbus*, says it was Professor Carl Christian Rafn's opinion that the "VI days' sailing west of Ireland" which was given as the distance from Ireland to "Great Ireland" was "an error of the transcriber . . . from an original XX or XI or XV." I think it was by omission of one stroke an error for VII. The actual distance out of sight of land between Ireland and Newfoundland is seven days' sailing—1,050 miles.

Anderson tells this story (from the *Eyrbyggia Saga*) on pages 17 to 20 of his Preface:

It must have been in this same Ireland the Great that Bjorn Asbrandson, surnamed the Champion of Breidavik, spent the latter part of his life. . . . His illicit amatory connection with Thurid of Froda [River Frod] in Iceland, a sister of the powerful Snorre Gode, drew upon him the enmity and persecution of the latter, in consequence of which he found himself obliged to quit the country for ever, and in the year 999 he set sail from Iceland with a northeast wind.

Gudleif Gudlaugson, brother of Thorfinn, the ancestor of the celebrated historian Snorre Sturlason, had made a trading voyage to Dublin in Ireland, but when he left that place again, with the intention of sailing around Ireland and returning to Iceland, he met with long-continuing northeasterly winds, which drove him far to the southwest in the ocean, and late in the summer he and his company came at last to an extensive country, but they knew not what country it was. On their landing, a crowd of the natives several hundreds in number, came against them, and laid hands on them, and bound them. They did not know anybody in the crowd, but it seemed to them that their language resembled Irish. The natives now took counsel whether they should kill the strangers or make slaves of them. While they were deliberating a large company approached, displaying a banner, close to which rode a man of distinguished appearance, who was far advanced in years, and had gray hair. The matter under deliberation was referred to his decision. He was the above-named Bjorn Asbrandson. He caused Gudleif to be brought before him, and addressing him in the Norse language, he asked him whence he came. On his replying that he was an Icelander, Bjorn made many inquiries about his acquaintance in Iceland, particularly about his beloved Thurid of Frod River, and her son Kjartan, supposed to be his own son, and who at that time was the proprietor of the estate of Frod River. In the meantime the natives becoming impatient and demanding a decision, Bjorn selected twelve of his company as counselors, and took them aside with him, and some time afterward he went toward Gudleif and his companions and told them that the natives had left the matter to his decision. He thereupon gave them their liberty, and advised them, although the summer was already far advanced, to depart immediately, because the natives were not to be depended on, and were difficult to deal with, and moreover conceived that an infringement on their laws had been committed to their disadvantage. He gave them a gold ring for Thurid and a sword for Kjartan, and told them to charge his friends and relations not to come over to him, as he had now become old and might daily expect that old age would get the better of him; that the country was large, having but few harbors, and that strangers must everywhere expect a hostile reception. Gudleif and his company accordingly set sail again, and found their way back to Dublin, where they spent the winter; but the next summer they repaired to Iceland and delivered the presents, and everybody was convinced that it was really Bjorn Asbrandson, the Champion of Breidavik, that they had met with in that far-off country.

III

On the Trail of the Vikings

More than a half-dozen evidences point to the travel through or sojourn of vikings in various parts of North America. No one knows how many other similar traces have been destroyed or never reported.

The Beardmore Find in Ontario

On May 24, 1930, James Edward Dodd, a mining prospector, sampling a quartz vein, blew up a clump of white birches to save the labor of cutting through them. This was near Beardmore, Ontario, about six miles from the north end of Lake Nipigon. While digging out the earth with the aid of his fourteen-year-old son Walter, Dodd unearthed some pieces of rusted iron. There was a sword with blade about twenty-eight inches long, which broke in two while he was lifting it from the rock on which it lay; an ax with cutting edge slightly over four inches long, a size to have been carried in a viking's belt; and a bar about seven-and-one-half inches long. Thinking these pieces of little value, Dodd left them on the ground outside his camp. However, they were seen by others, and the word spread.

Between June 17 and 21, John Drew Jacob, game and fisheries overseer in the district, went to the site where Dodd said he had found the implements. He reported that he saw the impression of the iron rust on the rock. . . . The imprint of the sword was very distinct on the rock; so clear was it that you would almost think the sword had been imbedded in the rock. . . . The stain of the complete shape of the sword was very plainly marked on the rock. . . . The trees had such a wide root system that they would have prevented the planting of these relics there within a generation and I can safely say that they had not been uprooted for more than two months, or since the frost had come out.[1]

A year later Dodd said he believed the pieces were evidence that he had discovered "an old Indian cemetery." When Dr. C. T. Currelly, curator of the Royal Ontario Museum, saw the pieces he recognized that they were in the style of eleventh-century viking artifacts. He believed that there should have been another piece, and so he asked Dodd if he had found anything else. Dodd replied that "lying over the bar of metal was something like a bowl that was rusted into little fragments." What had Dodd done with them? He had shoveled them out. In 1937, Professor T. F. McIlwraith of the museum visited the Beardmore site with Dodd and found a scrap of rounded metal. In 1938, J. W. Curran and Dr. C. E. Eakins found another piece of rounded metal. Dr. Currelly assumed these rounded fragments were from the boss of a shield. Subsequently, Dr. Johannes Brøndsted identified the bar as the handle of a viking rattle. The rounded fragments were the remains of the rings of the rattle. Their roundness and thinness would have suggested a fragmented bowl to Dodd.

If sword, axhead, and rattle had been traded among Indians, they would not have remained together. The fact that they did was taken as evidence that a viking had died at that place. Perhaps he was lost, or more probably injured and sick. He died with his weapons on a ledge close to hand. His unburied bones would have disappeared completely in a few years.

[1] From signed statements by John Drew Jacob made in 1936 and 1937, given to Dr. C. T. Currelly, who supplied the author of this book with a copy.

A story was told by J. M. Hansen in 1938 that some viking relics of the eleventh century had been brought out of Norway illegally by a Lieutenant Bloch, and that these were left in the basement of a house into which Dodd had moved in 1931. Doubt cast by this story is invalidated by Hansen's saying that "the objects were not those in the museum." [2] The date of Dodd's moving was too late for Dodd to have found the relics in the basement before May, 1930.

Some doubt about the genuineness of these articles was created in the fall of 1956. Walter Dodd, adopted son of J. E. Dodd (who had died in 1954), told museum scholars on November 23 that the Beardmore pieces were planted by his father. When the pieces were "found," his father asked him to sign an affidavit. "I hardly bothered to read it and besides I was afraid of my father. So I signed it."

Walter Dodd then made a new sworn statement that he and his father arrived by train at the Beardmore whistle stop in the middle of the night, and in the morning his father "laid the iron pieces on the ground at the spot where he had been blasting some time before." The son said he did not remember too much about the site except that it appeared to be on a hill. "On the same day," he said, they had returned to Port Arthur, but his father had left the weapons at his cabin on the mine site.[3]

This testimony that the iron objects lay on the ground at the discovery site only a few hours during the one day is directly controverted by that given twenty years earlier by John Drew Jacob. Dodd's widow continued to sustain her husband's original story. " 'This!' she exclaims, slapping a copy of the affidavit, 'this here is just a little bit of—I don't know what to say—spite.' Walter only says, 'We didn't get along,' and adds that things started to go wrong when he realized he was adopted." [4]

Apparently intimidated by the prospect of the forthcom-

[2] Toronto *Globe and Mail*, Nov. 26, 1956.
[3] "Viking Relics Myth Exploded?" by Robert L. Gowe, in Toronto *Globe and Mail*, Nov. 30, 1956, p. 3.
[4] *McLean's*, Apr. 13, 1957, pp. 30, 31, 80–84.

ing account in *McLean's* magazine,[5] the museum authorities removed the Beardmore pieces from public display. An official of the museum wrote me his regret that he "must be so indecisive in this case, but the facts of the case do not admit of a clear decision." Yet even though the Beardmore find in itself is not proof of viking placement in Ontario, it cannot be omitted from the over-all picture. It should certainly be on display in the Royal Ontario Museum, labeled as subject to controversy. It is neither scholarly nor scientific to exclude it as a possible evidence of viking penetration of the St. Lawrence waterway and the Great Lakes region.

The Horse at Follins Pond

Bert Heideman, whose house is near the shore of Follins Pond, about twelve hundred feet west of the gully, wanted more back yard and had bulldozers dig into the slope behind his house to make a more extended level. During this operation, the shinbone of a horse was uncovered. We do not know whether it had lain just below the surface or under what depth of soil. It is a shinbone of *Equus caballus*, the modern species of domestic horse. This species was officially first introduced into North America by the Spaniards in the sixteenth century. But did the vikings bring a horse with them to Follins Pond? We know from the *Flateyjarbok* that Erik rode a horse to the ship when Leif sailed for Vinland, and Karlsefni brought to Vinland all kinds of domestic animals.

Bernard W. Powell tells what happened. Heideman showed the bone to Melvin B. Summerfield, who had been a student of Dr. Ernest Albert Hooton, professor of anthropology and curator of somatology at the Peabody Museum at Harvard. When Summerfield showed the bone to Dr. Hooton and told him it might be connected with vikings at Follins Pond, Dr. Hooton "confirmed the fact that this bone was the

---

[5] The *McLean's* article purported to be a review of the entire case, but omitted the testimony of John Drew Jacob and also Walter Dodd's story that the pieces lay on the ground at the discovery site for only a few hours of a single day.

cannon bone of a small horse and agreed with me that its condition indicated an age of 900–1,000 years." [6]

Unaware of Dr. Hooton's comment, Dr. William S. Fowler and Dr. Maurice Robbins, both with a background of much experience in excavating bones in Massachusetts, said the shinbone seemed to them very old.

Powell, who has the bone in his possession, says it is "osteologically, the enlarged third digit metacarpal," and describes it as having "an exostosis or bony enlargement," a "splint" which "is only vestigial and has no function." He gives the estimated height of the horse from which it came as 127 mm, which is 4 feet 2 inches. He estimates that the "length from the foremost part of the head hanging obliquely downwards is about 2 m," or 6 feet 6 inches. This very small size is that of horses in the Shetlands, Iceland, and Greenland. Powell says the bone is not fossilized, though unusually heavy, for some reason he does not profess to know.

Until and unless the horse bone is tested for age, by a process said to be very costly, the bone is no proof for the presence of vikings at Follins Pond. On the other hand, there has been no proof that the bone could not be from 900 to 1,000 years old. It may or may not be important evidence, and is therefore evidence which cannot be ignored, but is something to consider.

Yarmouth Stone, Nova Scotia

On a rock formerly close to the shore of Yarmouth Harbour in Nova Scotia, there are strange letterings. The weathering of the grooves of the letters shows that the inscription, which has been known for more than 200 years, is unquestionably very old. The rock is now in the Yarmouth Library. Because of its weight, 400 pounds, it was certainly not carried to the harbor by Indians, but was inscribed *in situ*.

[6] Bernard W. Powell, "An Osseus Find at Follins Pond," *Bulletin*, Massachusetts Archaeological Society, Vol. 18, No. 2 (January, 1957), pp. 32–36.

ᛚᚱᚲᚼ ᚱ ᚲᛏᚲᚲ ᚢᛃ ᚼᛘ ᛁ

1 2 3 4+5 7 6+8 9 10 11 12 13 14 15

ᛚᚼᛁᚢᛗ ᚴ ᚼᚱᛁᚲ ᚢᚾ ᚼ ᚺ ᛁ

1 2 3 4 5 6 7 8 9 10 11 12 13 14 15

Yarmouth Inscription with Transliteration

A 400-pound rock, found at Yarmouth on the southern end of Nova Scotia, bears mysterious letters which are copied here and numbered in the order in which Olaf Strandwold transliterates them. Mr. Strandwold suggests that it is an inscription to Erik the Red, carved by his son Leif.

The inscription letters have been variously called "Celtic runes" and "bastard runes," whatever that means. Their maker was obviously either semiliterate, forgetful of correct forms, or a deliberate and ingenious mystifier—a typical runemaster.

Olaf Strandwold's transliteration of the Yarmouth inscription [7] not only grew out of a scholarly presentation and explanation of details but is persuasive visually when set beneath the original letters:

The 4th rune is a bind-rune, two letters (4th and 5th in Strandwold's transliteration) run together, a not-infrequent practice in runic inscriptions. The 6th and part of the 7th letters appear to be in reverse order on the Yarmouth Stone. Strandwold's reading of r (8th letter in his transliteration) is supported in its context.

From his transliteration, Strandwold translates the inscription:

Leif to Erik Raises [this]

This translation fits perfectly with the saga account of Leif Erikson's naming Markland (Forestland) "in accordance

[7] Norse Runic Inscriptions Along the Atlantic Seaboard.

with its nature," and with the assumption that he may have left an inscription as an ironic monument to his father.[8]

Runestones in New England

Several stones bearing runic inscriptions have been found in New England and have excited undue attention. Miss Frances Healey of Hampton Falls, New Hampshire, found one, apparently a grave marker, in 1933 when looking for stepping-stones for a garden walk. She found the runestone at the end of the door walk to the house in which her family had lived for 150 years. The stone is 8 inches by 11 inches and weighs thirty-three pounds. Miss Healey had no idea where the stone was discovered by the ancestor who had set the stone in the door walk. Possibly it had been picked up from a viking cemetery in Greenland by a New England ship captain and brought home as a curio. Most runic inscriptions in Scandinavia and elsewhere were on gravestones. The Healey stone is light enough in weight to have been readily transported.

Another runestone warrants closer attention. This is the Aptucxet Runestone, venerated by the Indians at the western end of Cape Cod. When those Indians were Christianized, they used it as a doorstep to their meetinghouse. Too heavy to have been loaded by hand as ballast, it weighs several hundred pounds. We may be sure that Indians never carried it very far. Strandwold's translation of its inscription is "Jesus amply provides for us here and in heaven."

About 1920, a hired man, a Ruthenian named John, saw and copied a runic inscription on a farm southwest of North Tisbury in Martha's Vineyard. He gave the copy to his employer, a Mr. Priester, telling him that the inscription was at a place from which one could see both Vineyard Sound and the ocean. Priester, now deceased, never saw the inscribed rock. In 1943, a copy of Priester's copy was sent to H. R. Holand by some friends of his who knew of his interest in runes.

[8] See my book *Atlantic Crossings Before Columbus*, pp. 204–7.

Holand and I searched the Priester woods. On another occasion I encountered terrible vines, but finally found a spot on a hill from which I could see water in both directions. There was no inscription stone, but many rocks had been quarried away and others incorporated into the retaining wall for a pond. The inscription will probably never be found.

The five runic letters as given in the copy made from the Priester copy were *th f l i m*. These do not make sense and are presumably incorrectly recorded. Holand saw that very slight changes in the runes would spell *Th o l e v*, which was a common name. Whatever the original letters were, it seems probable that there was a runic inscription on Martha's Vineyard.

A Runestone in Oklahoma

About a mile northeast of Heavener in eastern Oklahoma, on the southwest face of Poteau Mountain, 400 feet above the valley, is a huge flat rock bearing a runic inscription. The rock fell from a semicircular wall, a cirque formed by a waterfall in a past geological era, and landed almost upright, with one face almost due west. Judging from its size, the slab must weigh thirty-five or forty tons, for its exposed surfaces stand twelve feet above ground. The western face is ten feet wide. The rock is two feet thick, with six or eight feet of still-attached layers at its base on the uphill side. The inscription was certainly carved at the site.

The rock is from a lower ledge in the Warner sandstone member of the McAlester formation, Pennsylvanian in age. It is so hard that only with the greatest difficulty can it be broken by a geologist's hammer. A very fine-grained sandstone indurated with silica cement, it is extremely resistant to erosion. It is dissolved very little by chemical action. In any event, the rock lies in a high-walled valley protected from most winds, its inscribed surface several feet above any possible floodwaters. At this latitude there is little frost or ice expansion in the grooves—which on the vertical surface are

Runestone in Oklahoma

X	↑	⦷	⊢	M	⋈	F	↑
1	2	3	4	5	6	7	8
G	A N	O	M	E	D	A	T L

Continental Germanic futhork

f u th o r k g w(v) h n i y(j)	ᚠᚢᚦᚨᚱᚲᚷᚹᚺᚾᛁᛃ	e p s t b e ng d l m o a	ᛖᛈᛊᛏᛒᛖᛜᛞᛚᛗᛟᚨ

A huge stone slab near Heavener, Oklahoma, is engraved with runic writing used in Europe 200 years before Leif Erikson's time. Viking adventurers may have entered the Gulf of Mexico, sailed up the Mississippi River, and turned off into the Arkansas River.

quickly drained of water. Though slow erosion has rounded the angles that the V-shaped inscription grooves make with the rock face, the angles show no color change. The geological evidence all points to very great age for the inscription.

The inscription existed in 1830, according to the Choctaw Indians, and was of unknown origin. C. P. Kemmerer discovered it in 1912, and when Mrs. J. Ray Farley saw it later, she noted that the surfaces of the inscription grooves were covered with lichen. It would take at least a hundred years for that much lichen to grow.

The rock has been examined by three geologists: Dr. Mildred Frizzell, geologist of the State University of Oklahoma; Dr. William E. Ham, associate director of the Oklahoma Geological Survey; and Louis Desjardins, a consulting geologist for oil companies. These geologists find nothing to controvert belief that the inscription could have been carved from 1,000 to 1,500 years ago.

With runic lettering averaging seven to eight inches in length, and broadly and deeply carved, the inscription extends across the west face of the rock at the height of a man's shoulder. When was it made? Who made it? How did the maker get there? What does the inscription say?

The runic forms point to centuries preceding Leif Erikson. Six of the eight letters are unquestionably in the early Germanic runic alphabet. Form 8 appears in five or more inscriptions dated from the late fourth to the early sixth centuries. Form 2 may or may not be the one used in a fifth-century inscription on the Stenstad rock. The argument turns on whether there is or is not a short crack in the Stenstad rock. If it is a crack in the rock which seems to carry the upward diagonal stroke across and upward to the right of the vertical stroke, then rune 2 is undeniably present in the Stenstad.

The 2d letter of the Heavener inscription is A, or if it is an inverted or reversed form, it is N. The 8th letter is T, or if retrograde or reversed, it is L. The 1st letter could be an erroneous form intended for N.

Who engraved the Heavener inscription? The runic forms, with the two possible exceptions, were early "Continental Germanic." They were used in Germany, the British Isles, Scandinavia, Russia, and in many European countries from the fourth to the ninth centuries. Although the forms indicate the period during which the inscription was presumably made, they do not reveal the nationality of the maker. The Spanish under Coronado reached what is now Oklahoma in 1541, but did not come within many miles of Heavener. The French, who based claims upon La Salle's exploration of the Mississippi, sent an expedition into "Louisiana" in 1719, and a Swede, a Captain Bossu, traveled through that part of North America, and was given a post "500 leagues from New Orleans" on the Illinois River and not, it seems, within hundreds of miles of Heavener. But it is unlikely that any of these people, had they reached Heavener, would have employed runic forms so long out of use.

In this connection, there is an interesting statement in *Land to the West,* by Geoffrey Ashe, a book published in 1962 before the author knew about the Heavener inscription. Ashe argues that Europeans with beards must have reached Central America in ancient times and served as models for the stone gods with beards carved by Indians who have no beards. Ashe says his study convinced him that Norsemen or vikings must have entered the Gulf of Mexico perhaps 200 years before the days of Leif Erikson.

Vikings in the ninth century may very well have crossed the Atlantic in unrecorded voyages and rounded the tip of Florida into the Gulf of Mexico and found the mouth of the Mississippi. Since it was the viking habit to ascend rivers, it would not be surprising if the unknown party went up the Mississippi River, turned westward into the Arkansas River, and thence into the Poteau River to within three and one-half miles of the Heavener runestone site. Travel by boat in rivers for immense distances is easy. But the viking party had also to cross the Atlantic. To do this in skin boats would not be easy. It is therefore more likely that the vikings crossed in ships of viking times.

What does the inscription say? It can be read as Gaomedat, Gaomedal, Gnomedat, Gnomedal, or Nomedal. Some think it was cut for a "lark," and is a man's name, "G. Nomedal," but the first-name initial is too modern a reading, and there is no period or extra space after the G. Nomedal is no name of any known man in Norwegian history, but there is a "Numedal," a valley (dale) in the east of Norway, with a river, Naum or Nauma, from Naumar, meaning "narrow." The translations which now seem to me likeliest are Gaomedat ("Give attention to this"), Gnomedal ("Sundial Valley"),

and one with religious significance suggested by Erich Stirne-
mann, using, as was often done in runic writing, the name of
each rune: "Give Supplication God Man Before Day Has
Set."

Runic Inscriptions in West Virginia

Two runic inscriptions of the viking period were dug up
in West Virginia, 93 years and 85 miles apart. One was unearthed in 1838 in the Grave Creek Indian mound at Mounds-
ville, and the other in 1931 near Triplet Creek in Braxton
County. The Grave Creek inscription was on a small tablet
only 1⅞ inches long, and the Braxton tablet is 4¾ inches
long.

The mammoth Grave Creek mound was 295 feet in
diameter and 69 feet in height. The rings of a large oak that
stood at the top of the tumulus showed that the tree was 500
years old, and this put the era of abandonment of the mound
building back to about A.D. 1500. Curiosity and the hope of
finding concealed treasure led to the digging of a horizontal
shaft into the mound and the sinking of a vertical shaft from
the top. The finding of the tablet in the "upper vault" of the
mound is attested by five witnesses: Aberlard Tomlinson,
Thomas Biggs, Dr. James W. Clemens, Peter Catlett, and
J. E. Wharton. The tablet had obviously been in the possession
of Indians, who may have carried it to the site from many
hundreds of miles away.

There are two theories about how the runic inscriptions
of the viking period got into West Virginia. One holds that
the inscriptions were brought there or made there by vikings
who came up the Mississippi and Ohio rivers and explored
streams such as the Little Kanawha River and Triplet Creek.
Both tablets mention an "island," and there are islands in the
Ohio. This theory, however, seems less likely than the second.
This holds that they were carried by Indians. They may have
been transported to West Virginia from the region of the
Great Lakes by the Erie or Huron Indians, from Pennsylvania

by the Delaware Indians, or from southern Pennsylvania, Kentucky, or New Jersey by the Shawnee Indians, or possibly by Indian traders.

The inscriptions use letters from the early futhark and also have the Christian cross. The Grave Creek inscription was patently made at a time when Christianity was new and struggling against the religion of Thor, as is shown by the combined Christ Cross and Thorhammer. A "hodd" was a sanctuary that hoarded holy things.

Snails as Witnesses

Evidence of a very different kind pointing to the presence of vikings in North America comes from a lowly animal, *Littorina littorea*. This snail is now found along our continental coast near Halifax. There is, however, no fossil evidence of the species from interglacial or preglacial times in North America, according to Nils Spjeldnaes and Kari E. Henningsmoen of the University of Oslo. They believe that the species could have migrated to North America from Europe only during the warm postglacial period. At that time the mollusk was found in Spitsbergen, and conditions were similar enough in Greenland. But there are no fossil remains from this period in Greenland. More likely, the mollusk was carried to North America in viking ships.[9] People once thought that the Halifax mollusk population was introduced by ships from Europe in the nineteenth century. This is ruled out by recent radiocarbon dating of fossil shells from Halifax. The dating indicates from A.D. 1028 to 1488—the median date, 1263, being nearly 200 years after the end of the viking period. Yet its presence in viking ships would not be surprising. A hardy species, this snail could have survived a long Atlantic crossing in the bilge of an undecked viking ship. The mollusk is edible and used as fishing bait.

[9] *Science*, Vol. 141 (July 19, 1963); Vol. 142 (Nov. 22, 1963).

A Round Stone Tower

Though viking efforts to colonize North America ended, descendants of the vikings visited the continent 250 to 400 years after the discovery of Vinland.

One evidence of this is the round stone tower on the hill above the harbor of Newport, Rhode Island. Built in a medieval style, the tower stands on eight columns. Its wall is slightly more than three feet thick. The tower had a first floor over twelve feet above the ground, and another room above that.

The earliest historical reference to a round stone tower in America, brought by friends to my attention, is in a colonial paper of 1632 entitled: "The Commodities of the Island of Manati or Long Isle within the Continent of Virginia." This paper, which is in the Public Records Office in London, was intended to attract settlers to Sir Edmund Plowden's proposed Province of New Albion, at the eastern end of Long Island. People in the British Isles feared the hardships suffered by settlers in America and shuddered at the massacres of colonists by Indians. Before they would venture to start a new colony, they wanted assurances of sufficient food and adequate protection from the savages. The Plowden paper listed twenty-nine natural resources and conveniences that settlers in New Albion would enjoy, and called them the "commodities" of the region: vines, chestnuts, proper locations to build and launch ships and set up windmills, various kinds of fish and wild fowl, the fur trade with the savages, and "spring water as good as small beere." Also listed were mineral possibilities "on the continent northwards," and a bank "60 miles to the northwards," which was a good place to dry cod.

Nearly a third of the commodities showed prospective settlers how they could protect themselves against Indians. Obviously, since the Indians on Long Island would be contained by the Dutch at the west end and the proposed colony at the east end, it was a possible Indian attack from the continent that had to be guarded against. Thus, immediately following the assurance that "securitie . . . growes if order and disapline and intelligence with the savages . . . be had" in "New England on the North" (among other places on the continent), there came this statement (Section 27): "So that 30 idle men as souldiers or gent be resident in a *rownd stone towre* and by tornes to trade with the savages and to keep their ordinance and armes neets." (Italics are mine.) Section 28 specified that the "souldiers or gent" who occupied the tower were to be supplied by "25 souldiers and 25 marriners to trucke and trafficke by torne with the Savages, and never above tenn of them abroad att once in a pinnace planqued against arrowes." The tower was obviously already existing on the continent across water from eastern Long Island.

William Coddington and John Clark, who founded Newport in 1639, were curious about the tower and asked the Narragansett Indians about its origin. The Narragansetts were unable to enlighten them. Apparently they asked the wrong Indians. The Wampanoags may have possessed Aquidneck when the tower was built, for they claimed islands in Narragansett Bay, which they said the Narragansetts had taken from them.

The historian Benson John Lossing [10] says of the tower in Newport:

> On the subject of its erection, history and tradition are silent. . . . Governor Gibbs remembers the appearance of the tower more than 40 years ago, when it was practically covered by the same hard stucco upon its exterior surface. Doubtless it was originally covered within and without with plaster. . . . During the possession of Rhode Island by the British in the Revolution, the tower was more perfect than now, having a roof, and the walls were 3 to 4 feet higher.

The significant point in the first sentence quoted is that it was understood in Newport that its founders had made inquiries about the already existing tower.

[10] *Pictorial Field Book of the Revolution,* pp. 64–65.

The tower was an effective fortress, its first floor accessible only by ladder, which could be drawn up above the reach of enemy hands. The tower served as a fort, a watchtower, and probably also, as E. A. Richardson has demonstrated, a beacon, since the light of the fireplace would be seen through the low door in the opposite wall by any ship approaching the harbor landing. In addition to serving these obvious purposes, the tower was the beginning of a church, with a niche for an altar table and a well recess beneath it for sacred relics. Could the tower have been erected by Bishop Eric Gnupson who sailed for Vinland in 1121? It is unlikely that the bishop would have gone to Vinland before a colony had been established there.

The flues, with horizontal rather than vertical egress, seem to indicate about when the tower was built. No traces of chimneys (vertical egress for smoke) exist from Roman times. The Romans had hypocausts, or openings in walls, just above fireplaces. There are no chimneys in pictorial representations of Anglo-Saxon times. The danger of asphyxiation from smoke while one slept was provided against by the *couvre-feu* law in 1068, which required the extinguishing of fires at bedtime. This law was abrogated in 1200—evidence that in the twelfth century the invention of flues had gone far to eliminate the danger. In twelfth-century Rochester Castle in England there are primitive flues. The earliest mention of chimneys is in 1347, when chimneys in Venice were thrown down by an earthquake. The invention of chimneys had occurred some time before 1347, but chimneys appear to have been unknown in the early part of the fourteenth century.

From the above, the presence of the flues with horizontal egress in the Newport Tower would seem more indicative of a thirteenth-century origin than the second half of the fourteenth century. H. R. Holand believed that the tower was built by the Paul Knutson Expedition between 1356 and 1361, though he had no evidence for this. Although the Paul Knutson Expedition (see next section of this Appendix) may have had an ecclesiastical builder capable of designing the Newport Tower, the flues of the fireplace argue for an earlier date. Dr. Johannes Brøndsted's first impression of the tower supports his conjecture. After studying the interior as well as the exterior, he stepped back a little and declared: "This is in the style of the thirteenth to the fourteenth century. If this were in Europe, it would be accepted unquestionably as a thirteenth-to-fourteenth-century building. But it is in America. . . ."

There is a theory that the tower was built in the seventeenth century as a windmill. However, Lossing [11] tells of the windmill erected by Peter Easton in 1663:

This was evidently the first mill erected there, from the fact that it was considered of sufficient importance to the colony to induce the General Court to reward Mr. Easton for his enterprise, by a grant of a tract of fine land, a mile in length. This mill was a wooden structure.

Easton's mill blew down in a hurricane on August 28, 1675. Thereafter, a round wooden collar was attached to the off-round top of the stone tower (more than eighteen inches off the round), so that a rotating vane could operate, and the stone tower did duty for a windmill. But as Lossing says:

Its form, its great solidity, and its construction upon columns forbid the idea that it was originally erected for a mill; and certainly, if a common windmill, made of timber, was so highly esteemed by the people, as we have seen, the construction of such an edifice [the stone tower] so superior to any dwelling or church in the colony, would have received special attention from the magistrates, and the historians of the day.

Another reason we know the tower was not built as a windmill is that it contains a fireplace. Flour dust is highly explosive, precluding the use of a fireplace in a mill. The fireplace is clearly not a later addition. There are two flues, a few inches in diameter, which run up through the wall for a

[11] *Ibid.*, pp. 65–67.

dozen feet and then turn at right angles into horizontal exits. To have built the flues later would have required the removal and replacement of a whole side of the tower.

The dimensions of the Newport Tower tell us what unit of measurement its builders used. As all masons and carpenters know, dimensions of any structure are simple multiples of some standard of measurement, or are simple fractions of that standard. The linear unit used by the builders of the Newport Tower was about one third of an inch longer than the English foot, or about 12.35 inches. This unit was not English or Dutch. It was used in the Rhineland and introduced into Norway and Denmark through the Hanseatic League. By the thirteenth century it was used in Norway and Denmark, and later in Iceland and Greenland, until the introduction of the metric system.

The interior diameter of the Newport Tower was laid down as three fathmur (a fathmur being six feet and two-and-one-eighth inches of English length). The exterior diameter was four fathmur. Other dimensions reveal the use of the same linear unit.

The use of the Rhineland-Norse linear unit in the Newport Tower is not proof that the builders were Norsemen. They may have been Rhinelanders, or other members of the Hanseatic League, or, for that matter, anyone who chose to use the Rhineland-Norse unit. However, since there is evidence that descendants of the vikings did visit North America, and no evidence that Hanseatic Leaguers did so, it is more probable that Norsemen built the Newport Tower.

Runes and Artifacts in Minnesota

In 1898, Olaf Ohman was grubbing stumps with his ten-year-old son Edward on his farm near Kensington, Douglas County, Minnesota. They were working on the brow of a hill about 500 feet from the house of a neighbor, Nils Flaten, who came over to chat for a while. Ohman had difficulty with the stump of an aspen tree "about ten inches thick,"

ᚠ·ᚤöᛏᛏᚱ:ᛑᚴ:ᚠᚠ:ᛏᛑᚱᚱᚤᛏᛏ:ᛈᛑ:
8 göter ok 22 norrmen på
8 Goths and 22 Norwegians on

:ᛑᛒᛈᚷᚤᚤᛏᛲᛏ ᚠᚷᚱᛈ: ᚠᚱᛑ
opþaselse farþ fro
exploration-journey from

ᚤᛁ ᛏᛲᚷᛏᚦ:ᛑᚠ:ᚤᛏᛲᛏ:ᚤᛁ:
winland of west wi
Vinland over West We

᛭ᚷᚦᛏ:ᛲᚷᚤᛏᚱ:ᚤᛏᚦ:ᚠ:ᛲᛑᚠᚷᚱ:ᛏᛏ
haþe läger weþ 2 skjar en
had camp by 2 skerries one

ᚦᚷᚤᛲ:ᚱᛁᛲᛏ:ᛏᛑ ᚱᚱ:ᚠᚱᛑ:ᚦᛏᛑᛲ:ᛲᛏᛏᛏ:
þags rise norr fro þeno sten
day's journey north from this stone

ᚤᛁ:ᚤᚤᚱᛑ:ᛑᚴ ᚠᛁᛲᛏᛏ:ᛏᛏ:ᚦᚤᛲ᛭:ᛇᛒᛏᛁᚱ
wi war ok fiske en þagh äptir
We were and fished one day. After

ᚤᛁ:ᛲᛑᛇᚤ:᛭ᛏᛇᚤ:ᚠᚤᛏ:ᛩ ᚤᚷᛏ:ᚱöᚦᛏ:
wi kam hem fan 10 man röþe
we came home found 10 men red

᛭ᚠ:ᛒᛲᛑᚦ:ᛑᚤ:ᚦᛏᚦ: AVM
af bloþ og þeþ AVM
with blood and dead AV[e] M [aria]

ᚠᚱᚷᛏ ᛲ ᛲᛏ:᛭ᚠ:ᛁᛲᛲᚤ:
fräelse af illy
Save from evil.

᛭᛭ᚱ:ᛩ:ᚤᛑᛏᛲ:ᚤᛏ:᛭᛭ᚤᛏᛏ:᛭ᛏ: ᛲᛏ:
har 10 mans we hawet at se
have 10 men we have at the sea

᛭ᛒᛏᛁᚱ:ᚤᛑ ᚱᛏ:ᛲᛁᛒ:ᛁᚠ:ᚦᚤᛲ᛭:ᚱᛁᛲᛏ:
äptir wore skip 14 þagh rise
to look after our ship 14 days' journey

ᚠᚱᛑᚤ:ᚦᛏᛑ:ö᛭:᛭᛭ᚱ:ᛲᚠᚠᚠ
fram þeno öh ahr 1362
from this island year 1362

and he looked for the reason. Its roots were clinging to a stone thirty inches long, around which they had grown. He cut away the roots, and took out the stone. Shortly thereafter Edward called his attention to lines of markings on the stone, and Ohman got Flaten to come over and see what had been unearthed.

At first the neighbors thought the marks told of buried treasure, and there was feverish digging. Then after the stone had been put on exhibition in the window of the Kensington bank, the local folk recognized that the lettering was runic. That fall, O. J. Breda, professor of Scandinavian Languages in the University of Minnesota, published a partial translation, beginning, "Swedes and . . . Norwegians on a discovery-journey from Vinland west. . . ." Breda discounted the genuineness of the inscription, inasmuch as records of Vinland voyages never told of vikings from Sweden traveling in Vinland with vikings from Norway, and the language of the inscription is not old Icelandic but a mixture of Swedish, Norwegian, and (Breda assumed) English.

Breda's objections gave birth to a widespread notion that the inscription had been made by an immigrant who spoke a mixture of the three languages. Photographs were sent to scholars in Europe who promptly condemned the inscription because they said it contained the English words: *from, mans, of, dead,* and *illy.* Ohman expressed his contempt for the runestone by using it, inscription face down, as a doorstep to his granary.

In 1907, there chanced into the neighborhood a college student, Hjalmar R. Holand, who heard local talk about the stone and went to Ohman's farm to see it. In a letter to me,

---

In 1898, a Minnesota farmer dug up a stone that was covered on its face and one side with runic writing. Although some scholars consider the stone a hoax, it is more likely that it was inscribed by descendants of the vikings exploring the American continent in the fourteenth century. The translation is also shown here.

which the executors of Holand's estate have generously given me permission to quote, Holand tells how he became the owner of the Kensington Runestone.

February 20, 1954

The first time I saw Olaf Ohman I said nothing that might annoy him because I had been warned that he felt very sore that he was suspected of having faked the inscription. He told me of the stump with the flattened roots and the size of the tree. I said that that indicated that the inscription was very old, and he agreed, but added that the experts had come to the conclusion that the inscription was a fake, and, he added, "I suppose that settles it." To this I agreed because I then knew nothing about the contents of the inscription and had much respect for the scholars in Norway. However, it was a very curious find, and I thought it would be an interesting souvenir. I therefore asked Ohman if he would sell me the stone. He asked what I would give. I told him $5.00 whereupon he said: "Oh it ought to be worth $10.00 anyhow." I agreed that perhaps it was, but said I could not afford to spend more than $5.00, being only a poor student. I would like to have it, I said, because I had studied runes and Old Norse in college. To my surprise he said: "I guess you are just as poor as I am; you can have the stone for nothing."

H. R. HOLAND

Holand devoted himself to study of the Kensington inscription. He had a searching mind, a willingness to admit his own mistakes, extraordinary patience, and unfailing courtesy in answering his opponents, even those who descended to personalities and insults. In Skandinaven of January 17, 1908, he pointed out the misconceptions regarding the "English" words, and with understanding of the decimal numerals, gave a complete and accepted translation. He took the stone to France and to Norway, and showed it to geologists and chemists. Through the years, every word and every letter was subjected to scrutiny by philologists, runologists, and historians.

The Norwegian Society of Minneapolis appointed a committee to inquire into the facts concerning the discovery of the stone. In 1909, affidavits were obtained from Olaf Ohman and his son Edward, who said the diameter of the aspen tree had been "about ten inches," and from Nils Flaten, who saw the stone "covered with strange characters upon two sides," and

an asp tree about 8 inches to 10 inches in diameter at its base. The two largest roots of the tree were flattened on their inner surfaces and bent by nature in such a way as to exactly conform to the outline of the stone. I inspected this hole and can testify to the fact that the stone had been there prior to the growth of the tree, as the spot was in close proximity to my home. I had visited the spot earlier in the day before Mr. Ohman had cut down the tree and also many times previously.

A neighboring farmer, Roald Bentson, in an affidavit, said the tree was "8 inches to 10 inches in diameter," and he saw the flattened root. J. P. Hedberg, real-estate dealer in Kensington, wrote that he saw the stump of the tree and "the big root was grown as a bend . . . and could not have grown on side of stone. As said, large root run on top of stone." Four additional witnesses saw the flattened roots that had enclosed the rock. These were John and Olaus Flaten, sons of Nils, Arthur Ohman, who was eight and a half years old at the time of the discovery, and Henry Moen, who "saw the stump of the tree that grew above the stone."

The diameter of the tree was well established, and indicated an age of seventy years, and pointed to 1828 as about the time the roots of the tree began growing around the stone. The first white settlers came into Douglas County in 1858. Sievert N. Hagen [12] wrote:

No one can read the testimony without granting that the tree was eight or ten inches thick at the base. But in view of the controversy which arose about this, I am sorry that the stone was not found under the roots of a ragweed. It really does not matter

[12] "The Kensington Runic Inscription," *Speculum*, Vol. 25, No. 3 (July, 1950), p. 350.

whether the tree was ten years old or fifty. If it could have been proved that the tree was fifty years old, the authenticity of the inscription would still have been challenged.

In 1910, a committee of the Minnesota Historical Society looked into rumors that cast suspicion on Ohman and found them wholly spurious.

In the course of time every conceivable objection was raised against the genuineness of the Kensington inscription. While the many objections were being answered, it became apparent that what an "ignorant" nineteenth-century hoaxer would have had to know was too much for credulity. He would have had to know how to stimulate centuries of weathering of grooves carved on a rock. He would have had to know that the hill on Ohman's land was an island in the fourteenth century and until Minnesota settlers drained "the land of ten thousand lakes" and lowered the water level fifteen feet. He would have had to know that the five "English" words were Scandinavian words in the fourteenth century; that Swedes and Norwegians had been sent westward across the ocean to travel together in years that included 1362, the date of the inscription; that there was a waterway (Nelson River, Lake Winnipeg, Red River, and many connecting lakes) from Hudson Bay to the Kensington site; that a day's journey by boat in inland waters was seventy-five miles (journey during daylight hours); that a lake with two skerries lay seventy-five miles north of Kensington; that Kensington was fourteen days' journey from Hudson Bay; that at least ten runic forms not given in the published futharks of the fourteenth century were in use in the fourteenth century; that the pentadic, decimal system of numerals was in use in Scandinavia in the fourteenth century; and that Roman letters were in the fourteenth century creeping into use along with runes. In addition, a nineteenth-century hoaxer would have had to have imagination enough to create a composite language of the camp such as would have been used by Swedes and Norwegians who had for several years been living together in the wilderness. A hoaxer would have had to have the genius to create a text consisting of fifty-one different words, and thirty-five letter and number forms that would survive all the objections of linguists and philologists until, as is now the fact, every word of the fifty-one, except *opthagelse*, and all the thirty-five forms, except the *j* and the umlaut *ö*, have been proved to have been in use in Scandinavia in the fourteenth century.

Hagen shows that *opthagelse* "was thought to be modern because it is not found in Söderwall" (a dictionary of medieval words), and "because of a certain statement about the verb *opthage* in Falk and Thorp's etymological dictionary." He says *opthage* "would be more likely to turn up in an inscription concerned with a party of explorers than in law codes, homilies, or saints' legends." Holand presents very persuasive evidence that *opthage* was in use in Scandinavia in the fourteenth century.[13]

Only shreds of argument are left for disbelievers. Here is all they have to cling to: one word where the argument for it is better than the one against it; a runic form in which a slightly extended line would end debate; a runic form which minus one dot would be unquestioned. The burden of proof is no longer upon the defenders, but is now upon the skeptics —to prove that *opthagelse* and the *j* and *ö* could not have been used in the fourteenth century. This they are unable to do. All they can do is make assertions which they cannot prove, such as Dr. Erik Moltke's assertion that Petrus Ramus in the sixteenth century invented the *j* rune, to which Holand gives effective answer.[14]

In continuing to object to the *j* rune and the use of two dots instead of only one on the umlaut *ö*, Moltke is a stickler for textbook support, and those of like mind will agree with him.[15]

---

[13] *A Pre-Columbian Crusade to America*, pp. 80, 81.
[14] *Explorations in America Before Columbus*, p. 332.
[15] "The Ghost of the Kensington Stone," *Scandinavian Studies*, Vol. 25, No. 1 (February, 1953), pp. 1–14.

In any case, the maker of the Kensington inscription had no textbooks to consult. He was in the wilderness without benefit of such features of civilization. Recording the plight of his party, he carved in desperate haste—unlike the rune-makers in Scandinavia who had plenty of time to inscribe their tombstones with care. The Kensington runemaker was in terror for his life; he wanted to leave a record of the survivors who expected to be killed and whose best hope was that the inscription would be found and make known their fate. Americans are familiar with the misspellings of their own Colonial period and the grammatical shortcomings of pioneers and cowboys. So we are not shocked by the errors in the Kensington inscription. Scandinavian scholars, with an ocean-wide difference in point of view, were genuinely shocked by the violation of grammar and syntax. Moltke gave, as a reason for calling the inscription a "childish fraud," that *theno,* a neuter singular dative, modifies a masculine word *sten,* and in another place modifies a feminine word *öh.* Moltke wrote: "While the genuineness of the Kensington Stone is near to becoming a religion for certain Americans, a matter of national honor if one may say so, we here in Europe are not hampered by prejudices in this regard. . . . Remember that the language is our own, we know the language of the four-teenth century." Actually, some of the knowledge of the language of the fourteenth century, of which Moltke boasts, came to Scandinavian scholars only as a result of half a century of study of the Kensington inscription. To illustrate how that inscription has offended and revolted what Brøndsted calls the "philologically erudite" in Scandinavia, Moltke says the inscription "corresponds to 'The Kensington stone are a wonderful inscriptions, and we am prouds of it.'"

For the same reasons the American-Scandinavian scholar Hagen [16] says:

The inscription should be a perfect joy to the linguist because it is such a delightfully honest and unsophisticated record of its

[16] *Speculum,* Vol. 25, No. 3 (July, 1950), pp. 340–2, 351.

author's own speech. . . . His alphabet has the appearance of having been improvised from memory. . . . The total result does not
seem to have aroused much enthusiasm among runologists. . . .
A future generation of scholars will find it hard to understand how
an older one could have been so blind.

Fleeing from Skraelings, the members of the Kensington
Stone party were on the run. They and their slain companions
had doubtless brought destruction upon themselves, for if
they were members of Paul Knutson's Expedition (1355–63),
as seems likely, we note that the professed object of that
expedition was "death for the Eskimos, for the preservation
of Christianity." [17] Holand called it a "pre-Columbian crusade" and it did have a crusade's fanatic cruelty toward the
natives of America.

The pattern of mooring sites along the waterway by which
they presumably reached the island near Kensington is impressive. The unearthing of more than twenty-five iron and
steel weapons and implements, most of them within 100
miles of a central point between Cormorant Lake and Kensington, virtually proves that a Norse expedition reached that
area. Moreover, these artifacts were unearthed by the plows
of the first homesteaders—good evidence that they had not
been "planted" by immigrants. Of course no archaeologists
were present when the artifacts were unearthed, but that
does not give professionals the right to discount them all.
Filings from more than half the objects have been submitted
to the Carnegie Museum, which has undertaken a project of
metal testing by comparison with filings from weapons of
known medieval origin in Scandinavian museums.

The finders of so many weapons and implements over
nearly a hundred years could not have been in collusion. The
fire steel found at the mooring site at Cormorant Lake, the
lake with two skerries at a distance of one day's journey north

[17] Lambert Erkens, "Greenland, Yesterday and Today. Greenland's Catholic Past." *Bulletin,* St. Ansgar's Scandinavian Catholic League of New
York, No. 41 (February, 1943), p.7.

of the Kensington site, presumably has some connection with the inscription. The halberds, so light and thin as to be worthless for chopping, were not used as axes. They were symbols of royal authority.

The complete list, in the order of discovery, is as follows:

Object	Date	Place of Discovery
1. Fire steel	1870	Cormorant Lake
2. Axhead	1870	Cormorant Lake
3. Halberd	1871	Climax
4. Fire steel	1871	Climax
5. Axhead	1878	Republic, Michigan
6. Axhead	1894	Erdahl
7. Spearhead	1899	Trempeleau County, Wisconsin
8. Broadax	1910	Norway Lake
9. Sword	1911	Ulen
10. Axhead	1915	Brandon
11. Axhead	1917	Johnson
12. Axhead	1919	Thief River Falls
13. Halberd	1923	Alexandria
14. Sword	1930	Brooten
15. Axhead	1933	Mora
16. Fire steel	1938	Detroit Lakes
17. Boat hook	1938	Alexandria
18. Spearhead	1944	Lake Traverse
19. Halberd	1946	Mt. Vernon, South Dakota
20. Spearhead	1947	Alberta
21. Sword		Willmar
22. Spearhead	1961	Chohio
23. Fishhook	1962	Chohio
24. Axhead	1962	Norway Lake
25. Axhead	1962	Willmar
26. Spearhead		Oscar Lake

A final word is in order. We salute Hjalmar Rued Holand not only for his sixty-five years of devoted study of the Kensington Runestone, but for his magnificent reconstruction of the explorations made by the Friar of Oxford, Nicholas of Lynn, which he presented in *A Pre-Columbian Crusade to America*. Nicholas of Lynn, called "the man with the astrolabe," though in all probability not the inventor of the astrolabe, made one for himself at a time when the astrolabe was a novelty in England, and gave one to his king. However, in showing that Nicholas of Lynn was in Hudson Bay in the year of the date on the Kensington Stone, and that the expedition was there "divided," Holand wrote a new page in history. Nicholas of Lynn, with seven survivors of the "10 men" who had been left "to look after the ship," picked up Ivar Bardson in Greenland, and while the survivors and Bardson returned to Norway, Nicholas of Lynn returned to England. The story of Nicholas of Lynn strongly corroborates the events recorded on the Kensington Runestone.

IV

"A New World, as it were"

Henry, the first Sinclair earl of Orkney, was an explorer in North America almost a hundred years before Columbus. His father's ancestors were the dukes of Normandy and other Norman vikings; his mother counted among her ancestors the viking earls of Orkney and two kings of Norway.

Henry Sinclair was born in 1345, eight miles south of Edinburgh, the son of Sir William, lord of Roslin Castle, whose baronies included the Pentland Hills in Midlothian. Henry was brought up with the privileges of rank and title. The family at Roslin spoke French, and Henry, like every educated man of his day, was taught also to read and speak Latin. Pertinent to his story, because of what he was to find in North America, was something believed to be miraculous, though of course wholly natural a few miles from his birthplace. This was the "Holy Well of St. Katherine," the family's patron saint, from which flowed a never-failing "black oyle" which proceeded not from St. Katherine's bones, but was fed, as we know now, from a coal seam.

Henry's father on his way to the Continent could have posed in passing through London as the original for Chaucer's Knight in the *Canterbury Tales*, who loved chivalry and went to fight in Prussia. Sir William was soon reported slain, and Henry at thirteen became lord of Roslin, with a man's responsibilities. When he became of proper age, he was knighted.

The former earl of Orkney, Henry's grandfather, had

died about the time Henry was born. For a third of a century there was no ruler in the Orkney and Shetland islands who commanded respect for royal authority. Aware of the need for a strong leader in the two groups of islands, the king of Norway eventually chose Sir Henry, who could be trusted to be faithful to the Norwegian crown. When Sir Henry was formally installed as earl of Orkney in 1379, he was thirty-four years of age.

As lord of Roslin and owner of large baronies in Scotland, Earl Sinclair continued to give allegiance to the kings of Scotland, his close relatives; and at the same time as the earl of Orkney he fulfilled all his duties to the crown of Norway. The islands were a buffer zone between Norway and Scotland, with Norway hoping to retain the islands permanently against Scottish ambitions and encroachments.

Although Earl Sinclair had legal authority over the islands, in actual fact he had to make himself master of them by show or use of force. There were 170 islands, 53 of them inhabited, in a sea dominion covering thousands of square miles. By a document separate from his feudal investiture, Earl Sinclair was required to make two payments of "200 nobles of good gold [equivalent to about $3,000] at Pentecost next and Michaelmas thereafter" at Kirkwall, the principal town on the main island of the Orkneys. This made it compulsory for him to be in physical possession of the main island. He could not be merely nominal earl, but must be actual ruler by personal presence in that island much of the time. And so he entered the Orkneys, established residence at Kirkwall, and with sagacity, fair dealing, and force of personality made himself the actual ruler. He became in essence an independent prince, having power to make laws, coin money, and so forth. As earl of Orkney he became an elector of the kings of Norway.

To put down piracy among the many islands of the Orkney group and to protect fisherfolk therein, he had of necessity to build up an effective navy. This he was able to do because his baronies supplied the needed timber. In Norway shipbuilding had all but ceased. The wasteful method of hand axing, which produced only two planks from one log, required sixty oak trees to make one medium-sized ship. This had exhausted the stand of oak and pine. As a result, Earl Sinclair ultimately had a larger fleet than Norway's, though he never used his superior naval power against Norway.

It was some years before the Norwegian court felt that Earl Sinclair's naval strength was sufficient for him to extend his sway over the other group of islands in his earldom, the Shetlands. There the inhabitants had been more rebellious than those in the Orkneys against the Norwegian king's law. In 1389, Earl Sinclair was required to pledge himself to make four payments of gold at Thingwall, in the very middle of the main island of the Shetlands on August 10 in each of four years beginning in 1390. His signing of this bond required him to invade the Shetland Islands with naval and military force and to take actual possession of the main island, against what promised to be serious opposition.

Thus it was that in the summer of 1390, Earl Sinclair set out with his navy and soldiers in an expedition to take possession of the Shetlands. He landed first on Fer Island ("Sheep Island"), which was under the control of the main island of Shetland and lay halfway between the Orkneys and the Shetlands. There it was reported to Earl Sinclair that a foreign ship was being swept in upon a reef and was about to be wrecked. Prince Henry hastened to the scene and saved the men on board from the predatory natives.

The master of the ship was Nicolò Zeno, a nobleman from Venice who had sailed out of the Mediterranean to see the world. In gratitude to Prince Henry for saving his life, he gave him intimate knowledge of the two-masted fore-and-aft rig by which a ship could sail effectively into the wind. He also taught him how to install cannon on ships and shoot them without interfering with steering.

Nicolò and his men joined Prince Henry's navy and in fact saved it from shipwreck off the west coast of the Shetlands' main island. Earl Sinclair acknowledged that with-

Engroneland   Greenland
on Zeno Map   from Modern Atlas

Henry Sinclair, earl of Orkney, appointed a Venetian, Nicolò Zeno, as admiral of his fleet. Nicolò sent to Venice for his brother Antonio, who went exploring with Sinclair and many years afterward wrote the earl's biography. This map of Greenland, copied from one found with Antonio's writings, is shown beside a modern map. They are surprisingly alike.

out Nicolò's assistance he would have failed to subdue resistance in the island. To reward Nicolò, he knighted him and made him admiral of the fleet. Earl Sinclair built a fort in the harbor sheltered by Bressay Island (now Lerwick, the center of important fisheries), and soon established the king's law throughout the Shetlands. Nicolò sent for his brother Antonio in Venice to join him, and Antonio arrived the next year. In 1394, Nicolò sailed up the east coast of Greenland to the monastery of Friars Preachers (Black Friars) whose church, dedicated to St. Thomas, lay close to a small volcano. The church and monastery were heated by piped-in water from a hot spring. Several archaeologists, among them Alwin Pedersen, Helge Larsen, and Lauge Koch, have in the past half century established the existence of hot springs and formerly active volcanoes between 72° and 75° North latitude on the east coast of Greenland. Dr. William Herbert Hobbs,[1]

[1] "Zeno and the Cartography of Greenland," *Imago Mundi*, Vol. 6 (Stockholm, 1949), p. 15–19.

a geologist of the University of Michigan, identified the region in which Nicolò found the monastery as Gael Hamke Bay at about 74° North. Referring to what Nicolò described as a populous settlement of Eskimos, monastery, volcano, hot springs, and harbor kept free of ice by the hot water, Dr. Hobbs said: "Evidence for all these has been found there." Dr. Luka Jelíc tells us that in 1329 collectors sent out by Pope John XXII reported two ecclesiastical centers in "Grotlandia," one called Gardensi (Gardar) and the other Pharensi (the name suggesting the glow of the volcano like a lighthouse or pharos).

After Nicolò returned, he became sick and died. Antonio then became admiral of Prince Henry's fleet.

In 1394, Bishop Henry of Greenland was ordered to be exchanged with Bishop John of Orkney. An Orkney ship was probably used to notify Bishop Henry and take him to Orkney. There is no record of Bishop John's having gone to Greenland. Bishop Henry, who had been at Gardar from 1386, probably brought to Prince Henry a fairly accurate map of Greenland. If years later after Prince Henry's death Antonio found the map, he naturally assumed that the prince should be credited with having explored "the coasts of both sides of Greenland."

In 1397, an Orkney fisherman came home from having spent twenty-six years on the western side of the Atlantic. He recounted his experiences. Prince Henry gave heed to to his story, and Antonio, in a letter to his brother Carlo in Venice, recorded it.

The fisherman's boat had been wrecked on the shore of a great island called Estotiland. (From its position in relation to Greenland and from the contour of its eastern side on Antonio Zeno's map, we are certain that Estotiland was Newfoundland.) The fisherman was seized by the inhabitants. No interpreter could be found who understood Norse, but there was one "who spoke Latin, and who had also been cast by chance upon the same island." The island was "a little smaller than Iceland." (Actually, it is slightly larger, for Iceland has 39,688 square miles and Newfoundland has 42,734.)

The inhabitants possessed "all the arts like ourselves, and it is believed that in time past they have had intercourse with our people, for he saw Latin books . . . which they at the present time do not understand." They traded with Greenland in "furs, brimstone, and pitch." The fisherman remained in Estotiland for five years before he went "toward the south" to a forested land (Nova Scotia) called Drogio. (Antonio Zeno's original Italian was most probably *D'Roggio*—"of the reddish," or land of people of reddish color.) [2]

Beyond Drogio, the fisherman was for thirteen years passed from tribe to tribe as a valuable person because he could teach people how to fish with nets. He said that the land beyond Drogio "is a very great country, and, as it were, a new world" (*nuovo mondo*). This in 1397 was the first appearance in Europe of the term "new world."

Far to the southwest were cities with temples and idols [Mexico? Yucatan?]. The fisherman worked his way back to Drogio, where he spent three years. Here by good luck he heard from the natives that some boats had arrived off the coast, and full of hope of being able to carry out his intention, he went down to the seacoast, and to his great delight found they came from Estotiland. He forthwith requested that they would take him with them, which they did very willingly, and as he knew the language of the country, which none of them could speak, they employed him as their interpreter [in their trading voyages to Drogio]. He afterward traded in their country [Estotiland] to such good purpose that he became very rich, and fitting out a vessel of his own, returned to Frislanda, and gave an account of that most wealthy country to this nobleman [Sinclair]. The sailors, from having had much experience in strange novelties, gave full credence to his statements.

Fishermen have a reputation for tall tales and their stories are likely to be discounted as imaginative and boastful. It seems a safe guess, however, that fishermen through the cen-

[2] Gerald H. Morin of Nashua, N.H., says Drogio was "phonetic for Old Norman (*Des + Rougeaux*) as spelled by a Venetian."

turies discovered or visited many lands, knowledge of which never reached university scholars, who might have preserved the facts in writing and embellished them with fanciful maps. Henry Sinclair was not tucked away in a medieval campus but was in close touch with his Orkney Islanders, and he was confident that the fisherman was not lying, would not lie to his prince, but was telling literal truth. Prince Henry in his many meetings with the leading men in Scandinavia had undoubtedly heard of lands to the southwest of Greenland discovered in viking times, and the fisherman corroborated what he had heard.

The Kalmar Act of Union in 1397 had brought promise of peace, and Prince Henry Sinclair had no pressing military or political problems. By lucky chance, he had the ships, the money, the time, and the inclination prerequisite for transatlantic exploration. It is interesting that Kalmar brought official sailing to Greenland to a complete stop, but that Henry Sinclair, in planning his expedition to the west, was not sending it to Greenland, but to Drogio via Estotiland.

On Nicolò's death, Antonio became admiral of the fleet. He went with Sinclair on an expedition to Newfoundland and Nova Scotia to find timber for shipbuilding. But when the sailors found that they were expected to winter in Nova Scotia they complained, and Antonio was commanded to take them home. This map of Newfoundland, called Estotiland, is copied from one made by Antonio. Beside it is a modern map. The two show about ten points of resemblance.

Estotiland
on Zeno Map

Newfoundland
from Modern Atlas

We can fairly read Prince Henry's mind. The fisherman had mentioned "woods of immense extent," and "a very rich country" and "fertile." Such lands were worth investigating, and so Prince Henry planned to send "a few small vessels." But he began to see that with possession of a new land with untapped timber resources near where ships could be launched, he could add materially to his fleet, enhance his power, and make himself "master of the sea." At the last moment he decided to take "a considerable number of vessels and men" with Antonio Zeno as navigator, and to lead the expedition "in his own person."

His voyage westward took about forty days—1,850 miles at an average of two knots. They came to a safe harbor on the coast of Estotiland, but the inhabitants would not let them land. "They sent ten men to us who could speak ten languages, but we could understand none of them, except one who was from Islanda" (Iceland or Shetland). He said the island was called Icaria, the land of the Scots (Irish). If the opinion of Eugène Beauvois is correct, as it probably is, the original form of the name Estotiland was Escociland, land of Scotti. The Scotti were sea-roving Irishmen, some of whom settled Scotland, which was named after them. The names in the Zeno narrative support the identification of Newfoundland as Great Ireland.

About two days' sailing distance southwest of Newfoundland, Prince Henry's expedition came to another country. They anchored in Chedabucto Bay, north of Cape Canso, Nova Scotia, and the next day, on June 2, 1398, they entered Guysborough Harbour and landed. From the top of the highest hill in the vicinity, Salmon Hill, they "saw in the distance a great hill that poured forth smoke." Sinclair sent a hundred soldiers overland to investigate. After eight days the soldiers returned and reported that "the smoke was a natural thing proceeding from a great fire in the bottom of the hill, and that there was a spring from which issued a certain substance like pitch, which ran into the sea." The geological identification of the site is absolute. The only place within a thousand miles where a brook of viscous pitch flowed down from the top of a hill across a burning coal seam at the bottom of the hill was at Stellarton, Nova Scotia. The soldiers had met many inhabitants near there and "reported also that there was a large river, and a very good and safe harbor."

Antonio Zeno wrote:

When Sinclair noticed the fertile soil, good rivers, and so many other conveniences, he conceived the idea of founding a city [settlement]. But his people, fatigued, began to murmur and say they wished to return to their homes, for winter was not far off, and if they allowed it once to set in, they would not be able to get away before the following summer. He therefore retained only boats propelled by oars, and such of his people as were willing to stay, and sent the rest away in ships, appointing me, against my will, to be their captain. Having no choice, therefore, I departed, and sailed 20 days to the eastwards without sight of any land; then, turning my

Sinclair stayed behind in Nova Scotia with a small party. He made such a strong impression on the Micmac Indians that the story of his visit grew into a legend about a great prince named Glooscap. After exploring the country, Sinclair left by way of the Bay of Fundy, shown here on the author's map. The wind carried him to the Massachusetts coast.

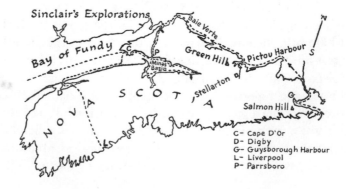

Sinclair's Explorations

Baie Verte

Bay of Fundy

Green Hill

Pictou Harbour

Minas Basin

S C O T

Stellarton

N O V A

Salmon Hill

C- Cape D'Or
D- Digby
G- Guysborough Harbour
L- Liverpool
P- Parrsboro

course towards the southeast, in 5 days I lighted on land [where] the inhabitants were subject to Sinclair.

Antonio's voyage from Nova Scotia to the Shetlands was at an average speed of three knots. In point of time, this is the last written account of a pre-Columbian crossing of the Atlantic.

Prince Henry in a small boat went around to Pictou Harbour near Stellarton, where he first met the Micmac Indians of Nova Scotia. The Micmacs were so impressed by his personality that their memory of his visit, and his spending one winter in their land, developed into a legend concerning "the first and greatest who came among us," a "prince," who lived at home in a town on an island, and had come from across the ocean via Newfoundland, and ascended a hill from the top of which he discovered another hill in the distance, to which he sent his men. The prince had a "sword of sharpness," and his men entertained him by the playing of "flutes." The Micmac chief became ambitious to marry a daughter of the handsome and powerful visitor, and inquiry yielded the information that the prince had "three daughters." These and other parallels between the story of Prince Henry Sinclair and the visiting hero of the Micmac tradition are too many to be mere coincidences. Prince Henry Sinclair and the legendary hero of the Micmacs are one and the same person.

The Micmac name for the prince was "Glooscap." They heard Sinclair's men call him Earl—"Jarl," with initial guttural. Since there is no *r* in the Micmac language, the "Jarl" became *Gl* and the sounds of the consonants of two syllables of "Sinclair" were retained in the *s* and hard *c* of "Glooscap."

After Prince Henry returned home, Antonio learned and wrote that he had "explored the whole of the country with great diligence." The Micmac tradition told of the extensive travels of Glooscap in Nova Scotia. From Pictou Harbour he went north to Baie Verte; thence by short portage across to Cumberland Bay; south by rivers with only a quarter-mile portage to Parrsboro; along both sides of the Minas Basin;

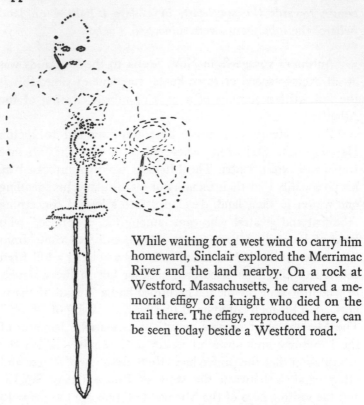

While waiting for a west wind to carry him homeward, Sinclair explored the Merrimac River and the land nearby. On a rock at Westford, Massachusetts, he carved a memorial effigy of a knight who died on the trail there. The effigy, reproduced here, can be seen today beside a Westford road.

west to Digby and by canoe route across to the site of Liverpool and return; from the Minas Basin to the autumn gathering of all the Micmacs on Green Hill west of Pictou Harbour; finally to the site he had chosen on the "portage" at Cape D'Or, where during the winter his men built a ship that had in it what the Indians described as trees (plural). Robert Barnett of Carthage, Missouri, has prompted me to say that a fourteenth-century, two-masted ship had a square sail and a mizzenmast with Mediterranean-type lateen sail, and it had also a spritsail at the bow. When the Micmacs visited Earl Sinclair in the spring, they were amazed to see his ship, were mystified because it sailed as by magic, and were struck with admiration of the skillfulness with which the hero had overcome his enemies, which were the darkness of night, storm, rains, the water, and winter. Sinclair entertained them at a great feast, spoke words of farewell, raised sail, and departed via the Bay of Fundy.

To sail out through the Bay of Fundy against the tide, Sinclair had to have a northeast wind, which carried him to the Massachusetts coast, where he tarried for a west wind to begin his return transatlantic voyage. Meanwhile, he explored, this time by small boat, up the Merrimack River and on foot up an Indian trail to the top of the lookout hill at Westford, Massachusetts. One of his attendant knights lost his life on that trail. Earl Sinclair left a memorial effigy of him on an open ledge of gneiss over which the trail passed. The most important lines of the effigy were made by rows of holes punched into the rock, but some glacial striations were imaginatively incorporated into the pattern. The knight had a helmet and a three-edged shield, and a great sword with punch holes to show it broken, as indication that its owner was dead.

The eyes of the figure are natural discolorations in the rock. The sword with over-all length of fifty-three and one-half inches is fourteenth century and a Scottish claymore in type.[3] The form of basinet points to the last quarter of the fourteenth century. The galley and other heraldic emblems on the shield point to some connection with Orkney.

The illustration of the military effigy is restricted to the certainties of the pattern. Those who examine the effigy (which is at the east side of the road a half-mile north of the library at Westford) may see more—or may imagine they do.

From the Massachusetts coast, Henry Sinclair sailed home to Orkney. He had only one year to live, for in 1400 he was slain in battle against English invaders. Antonio Zeno wrote a biography of him, but it was lost. Antonio's letters were in part destroyed by the childish hands of his great-great-great-

---

[3] In the Tower of London armorial museum is a sword "of the fourteenth century" with hilt two inches shorter than the Westford effigy hilt, and wheel pommel smaller, but blade the same length. Sir Archibald the Grim, third earl of Douglas, had a sword with seventy-four-inch blade.

grandson, Nicolò Zeno, Jr., who, however, after he grew up and regretted what he had done, in 1558 published all that remained of the letters, with a map. The title of this story of Earl Sinclair was *The Discovery of the Islands of Frislandia, Eslanda, Engronelanda, Estotilanda, and Icaria; Made by Two Brothers of the Zeno Family, Namely, Messire Nicolò, The Chevalier, and Messire Antonio. With a Map of the Said Islands.* Under the title of *The Voyages of the Zeno Brothers,* in the Hakluyt Society works, are the Italian original and English translation by Richard Henry Major. The chapter on Sinclair in *Atlantic Crossings Before Columbus* includes all the important passages in my own translation.

Although only portions of the record survived, it has been possible to fill in enough of the gaps to reconstruct the story. It restores to his proper place in history a great explorer who was a descendant of the vikings.

V

Chronology of Voyages

Voyages by Vikings

860	Naddod finds land (Iceland) and calls it Snowland.
c. 865	Gardar circumnavigates Iceland and it is called Gardarsholme.
c. 867	Floki the Raven sails to Gardarsholme, builds a house and ship-shed and winters there, and coins the name Iceland.
870	Ingolf settles in Iceland, and in the next 40 years, 400 families from Norway also settle there.
c. 970	Thorvald with son Erik the Red emigrates from Norway to Iceland.
982	Erik the Red discovers and explores Greenland.
983	Ari Marson of Iceland is driven by storms to "Great Ireland" (Newfoundland).
985	Erik the Red returns to Iceland.
986	Erik sails with 25 shiploads of colonists to settle Greenland. Eleven of the ships are driven back or disappear, and one probably starts the settlement at the northern tip of Newfoundland. Bjarni Herjulfsson sails from Iceland, sights three lands to the southwest of Greenland, and reaches Herjulfsness near the southern tip of Greenland.
999	Leif Erikson sails from Greenland to the Hebrides and to Nidaros in Norway. Bjorn Asbrandson sails from Iceland with a northeast wind and reaches a "great land."

1000   Leif Erikson sails from Norway to his home in Greenland.

1001   Bjarni Herjulfsson sails from Greenland to Norway.

1002   Bjarni returns to Greenland.

1003   Leif Erikson goes exploring, names Helluland, Markland, and Vinland.

1004   Leif returns to Greenland, rescuing shipwrecked people from a skerry.

1005   Thorvald Erikson sails to Vinland; next year explores Long Island Sound; the year after enters Somes Sound and is killed.

1008   Thorvald's men return home. Thorstein Erikson sails to recover Thorvald's body but reaches only the Western Settlement of Greenland.

1009   Thorfinn Karlsefni sails from Iceland to Greenland.

1010   Thorfinn Karlsefni with several ships and 165 prospective colonists sails to Vinland. In this and the followng two years he explores 2,500 miles of the coast of North America.

1013   Karlsefni returns to Greenland.

1014   Freydis, Erik's daughter, with Helgi and Finnbogi, sails to Vinland.   -

1015   Freydis returns home. Karlsefni with wife and son sails to Norway.

1016   Karlsefni sails from Norway to Iceland.

1029   Gudleif Gudlaugson sails from Dublin to the west and southwest to a "great land," where he meets Bjorn Asbrandson.

1047   Trond Halfdanson flees from Norway, visits Vinland. On return is shipwrecked on Greenland coast and dies. His body is taken back to Norway.

c. 1075   End of viking period.

Voyages by Descendants of Vikings

1112   Eric Gnupson, first bishop of Greenland, arrives in Greenland.

1121   Bishop Gnupson sails in search of Vinland and is never heard of again.

1189   A Greenland ship arrives in Iceland held together by nails of wood and whalebone.

1246	Bishop Olaf is sent to persuade Greenlanders to submit to the Norwegian crown.
1266(7?)	A voyage is made to the Arctic under the auspices of the Greenland bishopric.
1270	A clergyman retiring from Greenland brings home a description of Eskimos.
1285	Icelanders find land "to the westward off Iceland."
1289	King Eric of Norway sends Rolf to Iceland to seek "New-land."
1347	A Greenland ship arrives in Iceland with 17 men. It had been to Markland.
1355	The Paul Knutson Expedition sails to investigate conditions in Greenland, to exterminate Eskimos, and to rescue the lost colonists of the Western Settlement of Greenland.
1362	Leaving their ship in Hudson Bay, a party of Norsemen ascends the Nelson River and by way of Lake Winnipeg and the Red River reaches Minnesota.
1363	Nicholas of Lynn with seven survivors leaves Hudson Bay and sails to Greenland.
1364	They pick up Ivar Bardson in Greenland and return to Europe.
1371	An Orkney fisherman arrives in Estotiland (Newfoundland).
1376	He goes southwest to Drogio and beyond for 13 years.
1380	Four ships at the same time reach Greenland.
1389	The Orkney fisherman returns to Drogio.
1392	He reaches Newfoundland.
1397	He returns to Orkney.
1398	Earl Henry Sinclair sails to Nova Scotia. Antonio Zeno returns to Orkney.
1399	Henry Sinclair returns to Orkney.
1424	Claudius Clavus Swart, the Dane, visits Greenland.
1474	Pining and Pothorst sail to Greenland for the Danish king.
1477	A young Italian, Christopher Columbus, visits Iceland and picks up water-front gossip of land to the west.

Selected Bibliography

Anglo-Saxon Chronicle. Tr. and ed. by DOROTHY WHITELOCK. New Brunswick, N.J.: Rutgers University Press, 1961.

ARBMAN, HOLGER. *The Vikings.* New York: Praeger, 1961.

ARI THORGILSSON (the Wise). *Islendingabok.* Tr. by HALLDÓR HERMANNSSON, in *Islandica,* Vol. 20. Ithaca, N.Y.: Cornell University Press, 1930.

———. *Landnamabok.* Tr. by T. ELWOOD. Kendal, England: T. Wilson, 1908.

BRØGGER, A. W., and HAAKON SHETELIG. *The Viking Ships. Their Ancestry and Evolution.* Tr. by KATHERINE JOHN. Oslo: 1953.

BRØNDSTED, JOHANNES. *The Vikings. An Illustrated History of the Vikings: Their Voyages, Battles, Customs & Decorative Arts.* Tr. by ESTRID BANNISTER-GOOD. Harmondsworth, Eng. and Baltimore, Md.: Penguin Books, 1960.

DIRLAN, PETER B. "The Buried Farm at Stöng." *American Scandinavian Review* (Spring, 1961), pp. 44–48.

DYSON, JAMES L. *The World of Ice.* New York: Knopf, 1962.

ERKENS, LAMBERT. "Greenland, Yesterday and Today. Greenland's Catholic Past." *Bulletin,* St. Ansgar's Scandinavian Catholic League of New York, No. 41 (February, 1943), pp. 7–10.

FAIRBRIDGE, RHODES W. "Recent World-Wide Sea Level Changes and Their Possible Significance to New England Archaeology." *Bulletin,* Massachusetts Archaeological Society, Vol. 21 (April, 1960), pp. 49–51.

Flateyjarbok (often called "The Greenland Saga"), manuscript, No. 1005, fol. of the Old Royal Collection in Royal Library of Copenhagen. In making my translation, I have frequently consulted *The Flatey Book*, which gives photostats with translation. London, New York: Norroena, 1908.

GJESSING, HELGE. "Runestenen fra Kensington." *Symra*. No. 3. Decorah, Iowa: 1909.

GOODWIN, WILLIAM B. *The Truth About Leif Ericsson and the Greenland Voyages*. Boston: Meador, 1941.

Hauksbok (often called "Karlsefni's Saga"), manuscript 544, 4to, Arnamagnaean Library, Copenhagen.

Variant of *Hauksbok* (called "The Saga of Erik the Red"), manuscript AM 557, Arnamagnaean Library, Copenhagen. An English rendering of *Hauksbok* is in *The Norse Discovery of America* ("Anglo-Saxon Classics," Vol. 15). London, New York: Norroena, 1907.

HOLAND, HJALMAR R. *America 1355–1364*. New York: Duell, Sloan & Pearce, 1946.

———. *Explorations in America Before Columbus*. New York: Twayne, 1956.

———. *The Kensington Stone*, Ephraim, Wis.: The Author, 1932.

———. *A Pre-Columbian Crusade to America*. New York: Twayne, 1962.

———. *Westward from Vinland*. New York: Duell, Sloan & Pearce, 1940.

HONTI, JOHN TH. "Late Vinland Tradition (The Thorbjörn Narrative)." *Modern Language Quarterly*, Vol. 1 (1940), pp. 339–55.

HOWLEY, JAMES PATRICK. *The Beothucks or Red Indians: The Aboriginal Inhabitants of Newfoundland*. Cambridge: Cambridge University Press, 1915.

JELÍC, LUKA. "L'évangélisation de l'Amérique avant Christophe Colomb." *Congrès scient. internat. des Catholiques, Compte rendu*, Vol. 2, part 2 (1891); Vol. 3, part 2 (1894). New Haven, Conn.: Yale University Press.

KRAUSE, WOLFGANG. *Runeninschriften im älteren futhark*. Halle, Germany: Max Niemeyer, 1937.

LOSSING, BENSON JOHN. *Pictorial Field Book of the Revolution*. Vol. 2. New York: Harper, 1852.

MARKS, PERCY LEMAN. *Chimneys and Flues*. London: Technical Press, 1935.

MAYNARD, THEODORE. *The Story of American Catholicism.* New York: Macmillan, 1941.

MOLTKE, ERIK. "The Ghost of the Kensington Stone." *Scandinavian Studies,* Vol. 25, No. 1 (February, 1953), pp. 1–14.

Njál's Saga. The Arnamagnaean Manuscript 468 (*Reykjabok*). Tr. by CARL F. BAYERSCHMIDT and LEE M. HOLLANDER. New York: New York University Press, 1955.

NØLUND, POUL, and MARTEN STENBERGER. "Brattahlid." *Medelelser om Grønland* (Copenhagen), Vol. 88, No. 1 (1934).

PEIRCE, C. S. "The 'Old Stone Mill' at Newport." *Science,* Vol. 4 (December 5, 1884), pp. 512–14.

POHL, FREDERICK J. *Atlantic Crossings Before Columbus.* New York: Norton, 1961.

———. "A Key to the Problem of the Newport Tower." *Rhode Island History* (July, 1948), pp. 75–83.

———. *The Lost Discovery.* New York: Norton, 1952.

———. *The Vikings on Cape Cod.* Pictou, N.S.: 1957.

———. "Was the Newport Tower Standing in 1632?" *New England Quarterly* (December, 1945), pp. 501–6.

POWELL, BERNARD W. "An Osseous Find at Follins Pond." *Bulletin,* Massachusetts Archaeological Society, Vol. 18, No. 2 (January, 1957), pp. 32–36.

PUTNAM, J. PICKERING. *Open Fireplaces in All Ages.* Boston: Osgood, 1881.

QUAIFE, MILO M. "The Myth of the Kensington Rune Stone." *New England Quarterly* (December, 1934), pp. 613–45.

REDFIELD, ALFRED C., and MEYER RUBIN. "The Age of Salt-Marsh Peat and Its Relation to Recent Changes in Sea Level at Barnstable, Massachusetts." *Proceedings of the National Academy of Science,* Vol. 48, No. 10 (1962), pp. 1728–35.

ROUSSELL, AAGE. "Farms and Churches in the Mediaeval Norse Settlements of Greenland." *Medelelser om Grønland* (Copenhagen), Vol. 89, No. 1 (1941).

SNORRE, STURLASON. *The Heimskringla: A History of the Norse Kings.* Tr. by SAMUEL LAING, rev. with notes by RASMUS B. ANDERSON. London, New York: Norroena, 1907–11 ("Anglo-Saxon Classics," Vols. 7–9).

STRANDWOLD, OLAF. *Norse Inscriptions on American Stones.* Weehawken, N.J.: 1948.

———. *Norse Runic Inscriptions Along the Atlantic Seaboard.* Prosser, Wash.: Privately printed, 1939.

UNDSET, SIGRID. "A Saga of Greenland." *Bulletin*, St. Ansgar's Scandinavian Catholic League of New York, No. 41 (February, 1943), pp. 1–14.

ZENO, NICOLÒ. *The Voyages of the Venetian Brothers, Nicolò & Antonio Zeno, to the Northern Seas, in the Fourteenth Century, Comprising the Latest Known Accounts of the Lost Colony of Greenland; and of the Northmen in America Before Columbus.* Tr. and ed. by RICHARD HENRY MAJOR. London: Hakluyt Society, 1875.

Index

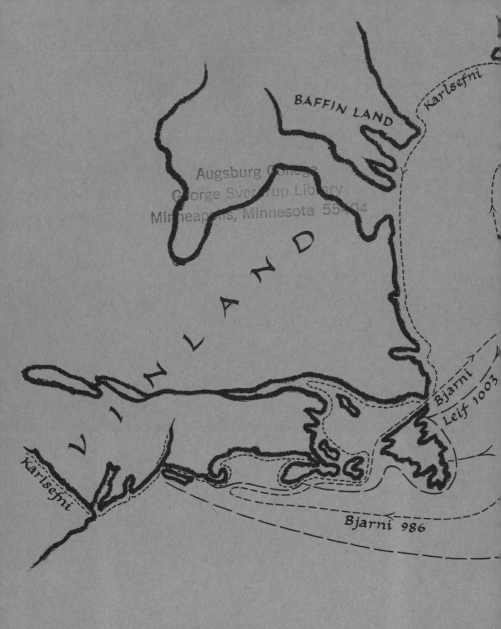

BAFFIN LAND

Karlsefni

V I N L A N D

Bjarni

Leif 1003

Karlsefni

Bjarni 986

VIKING VOYAGES